PRAISE FOR *ROCK NEEDS RIVER*

"Filled with intimate stories of lives intertwining, *Rock Needs River* is a marvelous ride through the complex creation of a family and the author's discovery that when things aren't like anyone ever thought they would be, all you have to do is just let them be that way, and somehow it will work."

—KJ Dell'Antonia, author of *How to Be a Happier Parent*

"*Rock Needs River* is everything parenting is—hopeful, devastating, emotional, all-consuming, life-changing, and at its best, capable of conjuring unfathomable bursts of joy. It's as honest and moving an account of family as I've ever read."

—Jerry Mahoney, author of *Mommy Man* and *My Rotten Stepbrother Ruined Cinderella*

ROCK
NEEDS
RIVER

ROCK
NEEDS
RIVER

A Memoir of a Very Open Adoption

VANESSA
McGRADY

Little

Published by Little A, New York

www.apub.com

Amazon, the Amazon logo, and Little A are trademarks of Amazon.com,
Inc., or its affiliates.

ISBN-13: 9781503903692 (hardcover)
ISBN-10: 1503903699 (hardcover)
ISBN-13: 9781503903685 (paperback)
ISBN-10: 1503903680 (paperback)

Cover design by Emily Mahon

Cover photo by Vanessa McGrady

Printed in the United States of America

First edition

To Grace,

This is the story of us. It is my story before I knew you, about trying to find my own tribe and figuring out the people in the family I was born into; it's an ongoing process for me and maybe it will be for you, too. We cannot untangle our stories; they are all woven in together, indelibly, unsimply.

I am writing this, in part, because I want you to know that I tried, as best I could, to keep a channel open between you and your birth parents. We have sometimes been close and sometimes not. How all that went down will become evident in the pages that follow. I'm guessing that someday you will ask more about it, and I will tell you the truth. Because we always tell each other the truth, and I want to feel OK about what I say.

You and I are so, so, so lucky that we've found each other in this big world. We are not perfect, but we are perfect for each other. I am telling this story because it is one of the best ways I know how to tell you that I love you and that I didn't do everything right on this journey, but I did the best I could.

And maybe, when we share our stories with others, they can take some solace that they are not alone in their happiness and sadness.

Love,
Mama

AUTHOR'S NOTE

This is a true story—or at least the closest truth I could excavate. I've changed some names in this book, because as much as it is my story, there's a cast of others seen through my lens. As far as the timing of events goes, sometimes things in real life happen like they do on a storyboard, one panel after the other. Sometimes you don't learn about events until days or years or decades later. Sometimes people obscure the truth. I've tried to keep this whole zany chronology and interweaving of lives as simple as possible.

SOMETHING I REGRET

You Can't Unslam a Door

I'd walked home from dinner with a girlfriend, Joanna. In the dark February night, chilly by Southern California standards, I saw two long, lean figures walking toward me, about a block ahead, right in front of my house. I knew who they were. I knew what they wanted. My mind went blank, and I threw myself, back first, into a nearby hibiscus bush. "Tell me when they're gone. Are they gone?" I pleaded to Joanna in an urgent whisper. Joanna craned her neck to see.

"They're gone, they walked around the corner," she said.

We continued on to my house. After a quick hug and a "hang in there," Joanna roared her white Porsche out of my parking spot behind my condo. I set about getting to bed and started drawing a bath. I ignored a knock on the kitchen door. The people had come back. I could hear them talking outside.

I settled into the bath, my visitors' voices and occasional knocks drowned out by the water splashing full blast into the tub. I turned off the faucet. The people were now talking to the neighbor on the steps outside my door.

This is the least relaxing bath I've ever had, I thought. I was cranky and resentful because it was a rare night home alone, without them and without my kid, who was at her dad's. This was my time. I didn't want to share it with anyone. My guts were in knots and I tasted bile in my throat. I wanted, more than anything, to not answer the door.

I thought hard. Could I wait them out? Would they just float away? And then I told myself to woman up. I stepped out of my still-hot bath and wrapped up in a towel. I took my time getting into sweatpants and a T-shirt. And then I went to the door and opened it, a crack, wide enough for me to put my face out.

There they were. Bill and Bridgett, with their matching waist-length ashy-brown hair, their matching worn jeans. They were bundled in jackets. I didn't make a move to let them in or open the door wider.

"Hey, what's up?" I asked. As if I didn't know they had been there for an hour. As if I didn't know that they wanted me to ask them in. As if we were casual neighbors. There was a pause, and it was clear I wasn't going to invite them in this time.

Bridgett extended her hand. "I just wanted to give you back the key from Meaghan's." I'd hooked them up with a house-sitting gig for an acquaintance, which had ended several weeks before. I took the key. "Thanks."

More silence.

"So what's your plan?" I asked.

"We're going to get on a bus to Texas in the next couple days. We might have better luck with housing from the VA there," said Bill.

"OK, well, good luck. Keep me posted. Take care."

I closed the door. They walked back out into the night. It was too late for them to go to the shelter, and I knew this.

They were—are—my daughter's birth parents.

I went back to bed. I was not comforted there, my normally warm and welcoming refuge from everyone and everything, with its heavy blankets and novel waiting for me on the nightstand, because I was the worst person in the world just then.

PART I

MISSING IS ITS OWN KIND OF MADNESS

One

Unlovable

For most of my twenties, becoming a mother wasn't on the immediate to-do list—the thought was squirreled away as something I'd get around to, eventually. The vision went like this: I'd be a Woman Who Had It All, with a husband and a house and some sort of massively paying and morally satisfying job for which I'd wear a sharp black Anne Klein suit (with a washable gem-toned sueded silk blouse underneath!). Each night I'd come home, happy and tired, to see my little one(s). I'd order some food for all of us for dinner (Chinese food delivery is a working mom's best friend, am I right?), or maybe Future Husband would have some artfully prepared leftovers ready (we would be loosey-goosey with traditional gender roles in our house!). As a family, we would take a wide variety of vacations, such as backpacking through Southeast Asia with nothing but a small tote bag, three sarongs, and our wits, as I'd seen a Maori family do once. We would be happy and complete and on track for an early retirement.

But this was all a very remote fantasy. There were too many things I still had to do—like figure out a career. In two years, I'll get serious about having kids, I'd tell myself. And then two years would come and go, and I'd say, In two more years, I'll get serious about having kids.

I worked in restaurants because that was the quickest (legal) way in New York to make cash with little or no marketable skills. As a young waitress in the late '80s and early '90s, my pattern was to work until midnight or two a.m., slap a twenty-dollar bill on a friendly bar, and then drink for free until obliteration, when everything finally shut down at four a.m. Once or twice (or maybe more, because heavy drinkers are unreliable narrators), I woke up in a strange bed, stinking of booze and sex and bewilderment. I even cheated on a serious boyfriend, Nick, a very cute bespectacled Yalie, whom I loved beyond infinity. Whose attention and commitment I wanted so badly that I thought, using some parallel-universe, warped sense of reason, that my infidelity would make me more desirable to him. But really, there just wasn't enough love for me in the whole world, and I knew this, and I would cement it with my actions.

Nick landed a job in New Mexico at the *Gallup Independent*, a small newspaper based in a tiny, gritty town amid several Native American reservations. I followed, first taking a position overnights at a radio station, and moving on to the same newspaper.

Within a few weeks of arriving, I realized that the copyeditor, Joy, a young Julia Roberts look-alike with a tinkling laugh, was capturing a little too much of Nick's attention. There was a buzz between them, thick with longing. She wasn't like that with me or any of our other colleagues. Only Nick.

His flirtation may have been a time-release retaliation for my indecencies back in New York. I'd confessed to Nick in hopes that we could have a clean slate once we moved and maybe get married someday. But Nick was, rightly, wary of me.

One evening, I picked up a message on our voice mail that wasn't intended for me. "Hey, boy," Joy purred. "Just checking to see what you're doing. Miss you."

For the next few days, I brimmed with rage and tears. When I could no longer contain myself, calmly, methodically, like a cool villain in a Bond film, I marched up to her desk. "I know what's happening with you and Nick. I'm miserable. I will make life miserable for all of us. I suggest you figure something else out." And then, within a couple weeks, she packed up her sensibly sexy oxfords and A-line skirts and moved out of town. Nick and I left shortly after, together but separately, driving north, him in his sturdy, little Volkswagen Rabbit, me in my hulking Ford F-150 with dual gas tanks, alternating two cassette tapes: Arrested Development's "3 Years, 5 Months And 2 Days in the Life of . . ." and Soul II Soul's "Keep on Movin'." I was glad that we were leaving, still somewhat together, but wondered what the point was. I'd felt committed but knew he wasn't—the little box I'd gotten from him the previous Christmas contained only earrings.

We headed to the Olympic Peninsula (or "OP," to the locals), in rural western Washington state, where I'd attended most of junior high and high school. The OP is where cows sometimes cause traffic jams, where bad coffee is a sin, where the dark and wet, wild weirdness has been used as the backdrop for *The Ring* and *Twilight* and *Snow Falling on Cedars*. I wanted to be closer to my grandmother Grace, who lay slowly wasting from multiple sclerosis, looking out over the glassy waters of Lilliwaup Bay, in a home her father built from the rocks and trees on the land.

Soon after the move, Nick and I broke up in painful, staggered spurts.

I worked as a waitress and freelance writer and cobbled together a down payment from a credit-card advance and my meager savings and moved into a cabin on five acres, off the grid. I installed solar panels and took a shower from an oversize kettle heated on my rusty iron stove. Water was limited to whatever I could haul in or catch from my roof and heat. Mostly, I loved being part of the natural world. I moved to the rhythm of the seasons, hunkering down with firewood and blankets and wine and tea in the winter, and celebrating the return of spring by moving my shower—a bag I'd fill with water warmed on the stove and hang on the outside wall—outdoors, and planting tomatoes, which grew surprisingly well. I became acutely aware of the water I used, the waste I generated, the coyotes that howled in the night. I was in a continual cycle of beating back the rabid blackberry bushes that threatened to engulf anything in their way, and marveled that Mother Nature has absolutely zero need for us. She will always find herself again. Once, a bear came into my unlocked cabin and took a shit on my coffee table. I'm still marveling at that.

Dating came easy. There was the Celtic Prince, a burly, wild-minded, watery-blue-eyed Irishman with a flyaway blond modified Mohawk (he shaved off "the grey bits" on the sides), whose real name was Alan, but he liked to call himself Rik O'Shea. We drank a lot together and did crazy things like park his old maroon Dodge van on the beach, then wake up and jump into the grey icy waters of the Strait of Juan de Fuca in the morning to wash off our beery sex stink. With friends, we'd sit around campfires and he'd bark out Christy Moore songs, slapping at his black acoustic guitar. We learned "Fairytale of New York," the rollicking, sad-sweet Pogues Christmas carol, and sang it together as our party trick. I liked his originality, his Irishness, his possibly true tales of camping with Central American freedom fighters of one sort or another. People such as Alan are always entertaining, but when you enter into a relationship with them, it's like trying to catch the business end of a high-voltage power line. It will be exciting, an exercise in agility and toughness. But when you do finally get a grasp, inevitably you will get burned, deeply, indelibly. He cheated on me with a construction worker named Monika and tried to cover it up by saying it was raining too hard to come home and he slept in his van. After one particularly volatile fight and a round of makeup sex, we were lying in bed. "So," he said, "will we get married?"

It was one of those times I couldn't figure out if this was a proper proposal or just another Irish idiom. No matter. "No. No fucking way."

I leapfrogged to the sweet and funny George, a sculptor I'd met at a party. He was so sensitive, tears would pool in his eyes as he described the plight of algae in a polluted world and the disruption of nature's balance. He was a nurturer, who fed me kale and tofu and made me organic tea and taught me the ways of herbs. We slipped into a comfortable coupledom.

The best baths happened in George's claw-foot tub, so I'd head over there every few days to get a good wash in. George's bathroom was large enough that he could fit a chair or two in there. One summer day, I was lolling around in the bath, and, inexplicably, with no apparent trigger, I wanted a baby. I was nearing thirty. I felt an allover tug in my body, a missing of someone I didn't know. Every single cell in me ached. The tears started dripping down my face, slipping into the bathwater.

I can't say why, exactly, I had the urge to become a mother. Probably from following the map I'd inherited from my own parents: a complex yet binary system of either following their examples or pointedly, deliberately doing the opposite. My Irish American father, Patrick, was the warmest, funniest, and smartest man in any room. "Come stay with us," he'd tell friends and family and even people we didn't know well. They'd join us at the table, and he'd lay out a spread (salmon, probably, or his throw-down dish, Moroccan chicken-couscous stew). He had a fully stocked liquor cabinet and a fancy Italian cappuccino machine and soda hidden "for company" so you could pretty much have any beverage you could think of.

He knew when and how to give hugs. His own father wasn't affectionate with Dad and his two brothers, and Dad once told me he made a conscious choice to be extra loving for us. Besides his booming voice on the other end of the phone, perhaps what I miss the most about him are those Paco Rabanne–scented embraces that seemed to go on for a small eternity.

But Dad was chronically late for everything, except for airplanes. (Airplanes don't love you. They are immune to your Irish charms and do not care a whit about why you are late. Your emergency is not their problem; your anger will not keep them grounded.) Growing up, I'd spent countless long hours standing around in the rain and cold and impending dark, waiting after practice, looking for Dad's grey Citroën, or the red one that came after, or the red Buick Skylark, or the pea-green Mercedes, depending on the decade. Helpful friends and their mothers would offer to give me a ride, but I knew if I said yes and Dad showed up and I was gone, the wrath I'd face wouldn't be worth it. I decided when I was small that I wouldn't be the kind of person who would be late. If I am early, I'm on time; if I am on time, I'm late. And if I am late . . . well, that hardly ever happens.

From Mom, a prolific artist and ethereal spirit, I learned to cultivate beauty. Even though I am in no way a visual artist, I adore the exquisite. I watched and learned how to make good soup as she does, by sautéing, then boiling up a bunch of vegetables, adding stock, and throwing everything into the blender. A Buddhist, Mom taught me that the Buddha-print skirt I'd purchased for her was taboo (you are not supposed to wear the image of him below the waist or as nonspiritual adornment), and I am, hopefully, more sensitive to things important to other people because of her.

My mother wasn't always on hand for the child-rearing; I got a lot of mother types who helped me to figure out womanhood. Through a string of live-in housekeepers who helped my father with logistics and childcare, I learned how to pick out my first high-ish heels; how to use eyeliner and to not load up my face with foundation, lest I look older than my years; how to party on a sailboat that belonged to a Roger Daltrey look-alike, an underemployed tennis pro.

Another mother figure, my aunt Corky, has always said "I love you" at the end of any phone conversation. I decided at nineteen that it was such a lovely way of being that I would also tell people I loved that I loved them every chance I got. I think a lot about those who left for work on 9/11 and never came home. Did they leave in the middle of a fight? Did they kiss goodbye? I think "I love you" covers this. Just in case.

My dad's longtime partner, Holly, was more of a day-to-day influence when she lived with us. From her, I saw that women put on Dave Brubeck, loud, on Sunday mornings and make a loungy brunch and brew fresh coffee; women wear chic flats and flowy, beautiful clothing; women have an undying devotion for their men, even when their men act like assholes.

Both my parents passed their love of humanity to me. They were so wildly incompatible with each other, yet at their core, so bighearted with a hardwired conviction about how people should be treated and things that were essential for a life well lived. Their coterie of eccentrics, artists, intellectuals, each of whom brought something essential to the mix, were funny or exceptionally talented or daring or outrageous, creative firestorms. My parents taught me how to create a tribe. Some of my blood-related family is in my tribe, to be sure, but most of its members I've picked up along the way, starting when I was four with my best friend, Lisa, who lived downstairs and who is closer to me today than any blood sister could be. My tribe is hilarious and loyal and helpful and made up of fragile souls and supersonic minds and great, big, fat beating hearts, and I wouldn't be who I am without them. My parents taught me how to find and keep people. And maybe, maybe, I could be a mom and bring everything I knew to a little soul, and we could love each other in a way only a mother and daughter could. Or should.

But as I was crying in George's bathroom in that big enamel-over-iron tub, there was a soft knock on the door. A local sorceress (Port Townsend is rife with those practiced in the ancient arts of magic and healing) named Ruby, whom everyone just called by her last name, Moss, had come by to say hello to us. She sat her mighty yet lanky frame down on the chair next to the tub, saw me crying, and handed me a cup of steaming tea. She didn't seem fazed by my nakedness, so I wasn't, either. I tried to explain my tears the best I could. She looked at me and then said, in all seriousness, "Yes, I know that feeling. I have that when the aliens leave my body."

I didn't know if she was talking metaphorically about her own children or actual aliens, but I burst out laughing, and she returned a slow, knowing Cheshire cat smile. Crisis averted, for a while, at least.

George proved to be a devoted mate, but I was feeling complicated and he was beautifully simple. So simple, in fact, that after several months everything he did, or said, or wore became an annoyance to me. Once, he donned a beyond-Cosby black-and-white cotton turtleneck sweater to wear to my father's for dinner.

"Do you have to wear that?" I asked, hating myself for saying it but letting the words tumble out anyway.

He looked at me, unaware of any issue. It wasn't so much of a wardrobe choice as it was a shorthand for who he was: unassuming, earthy, and without vanity or pretense. It was a sweater from the thrift store, probably the first thing he'd reached for that day without a thought except to its purpose, to keep him warm.

My focus on the terrible turtleneck was just a way to separate from him, finding something, anything, about this sweet, lovable man to resist. Soon after, we traveled to Mexico together on vacation and took a sunset walk on the Malecón of La Paz, looking out over the Sea of Cortez. The air around us was thick with "Will you marry me?"

Apropos of nothing we were discussing, I blurted out, "I can't marry you. I don't know if I'll ever marry."

While I liked the idea of marriage, someday, to someone, I had no tools. I'd received only negative messages about marriage from my father, himself twice married and divorced. One subtle cue came when I was thirteen or so, and Dad, brother Ian, and I were in a Mostly White-People Mexican place in a Scandinavian-themed town called Poulsbo, when a waitress, her blonde hair done up, blue eyes sparkling, bopped over to our table. Seeing the scarred battleground of crumbs, sauce, and food flotsam littering the table (we invariably left every restaurant table looking like some kind of heinous, violent food crime had occurred), she asked, pleasantly, if we needed anything else. We didn't. She put the check on the table and scooped up cash from my father. He watched her walk away and muttered, "With piano legs like that, nobody will ever marry her."

My horrified brain tried to process his words: you need to look a certain way in order for someone to love you. (Mental check: I'd inherited my mother's prima-ballerina slim calves, strengthened by my own dance, basketball, and volleyball pursuits, so I figured I was safe in that way, but my fleshy, waistless middle could cause a problem.)

"Dad?" I asked.

For Dad, Love with a capital *L* was the end game—it was good to be in love. It made you alive. It made life more sparkly and fun. I remember really liking one of his girlfriends, Carolyn, a tall, dark "nightgown model" who would play in the park with us. When she stopped coming around, I asked him what happened. "She wasn't smart enough," he said. I wondered who would be enough. Nobody, maybe.

But also, Love could fuck you up. When I was about ten, Janet, a witty feminist psychologist, broke his heart. He couldn't hold back the tears and sobbed all over the soft caramel-colored leather of his Citroën. I didn't know what to do but hold his hand and just be quiet with him. He loved that moment and talked about it the rest of his life.

But marriage. "That's only for when you want a family. And even then . . . ," he would say.

He believed deeply that marriage would bleed you dry in every way. He and the love of his life, Holly, were together for twenty-five years, yet they never married, though at times that was what she wanted.

George's eyes watered after my relationship-killing declaration. Any bloom of love and excitement he'd had withered instantly. "But I was going to propose on this trip," he said.

11

"I know. I'm so sorry."

We ate lobster in uncomfortable silence, waves lapping along the stone bulkhead, knowing that there would be nothing left for us when we got home. George would have been a great dad. I, however, would have been a terrible wife for him. Also, I didn't care as much about the plight of the algae.

And still, it would be a long time before I was ready for marriage, and the thought of having children seemed impossible and inaccessible for someone like me, scratching for a few bucks with waitressing and freelancing gigs, not quite having mastered the bucking-bronco bare-back ride of life.

Two

The Eggs and I

Having a baby transformed from an abstract thought to a delight-ful reality in 2000, when I was living in Seattle, working as an in-flight-magazine editor. My sore 36Cs busted out of my bra, my nose became bionic, I was nauseated yet starving for oranges. I was pretty sure my period was late, but I never bothered to track it much because I'm a Mary on the spot, every twenty-eight days. You could set a train schedule to my cycle. In a mix of panic and wonder, I reread the section on fertility from *Our Bodies, Ourselves* over and over again, and then went out and bought a pregnancy test, which confirmed that yes, there was a tiny speck of a person growing inside me. I was pregnant for the first time, which felt like standing on the precipice of a new universe full of love and adventure, a club where others had gone before yet couldn't quite fully convey the experience to those on the other side. From here on, I thought, I would be not just a journalist, not just a daughter and a girlfriend and a sister and a friend, but a mother, which would trump every other role to date. I would be uniquely positioned to give and receive quantum amounts of love, and it would be unlike anything I'd ever known. I would be more whole and join a legion of humanity that had gone before me.

My boyfriend, Shane, was much older—fifty-four to my thirty-two. He was an anger-management therapist by day and the impresario of an old-timey vaudeville show in our small town, which was how we'd met. He'd seen me in our community theater and asked me to join his ragtag troupe—he was a trained mime, among other things, and used his physical skills to revive old Ernie Kovacs routines and gags such as a very serious chanteuse singing "My Funny Valentine" to Shane, who was outfitted in a full gorilla suit. The show was a wacky, hyperlocal testament to our community's eccentricities. I liked his authority, his gravitas, his artistic determination, and his creativity. He had close-cropped, curly salt-and-pepper hair and moony blue eyes and kept his short body in good shape. He had a job and a car and a big, drafty farmhouse under perpetual construction, so Shane was, in our small town, a catch. He also had a son, Neville, who was starting junior high school. Shane was pretty much one and done when it came to kids.

We were on our three-peat. Shane and I had broken up twice before. A psychic had told me that Shane and I had had many past lives together as brother and sister and husband and wife, each of us alternating between male and female. In our last life together, she said, we were bakers. But there was something we were still trying to work out across time and generations, never quite getting it right. That felt eerily accurate to me.

I loved curling up on his antique overstuffed couch and perusing a musty, old, esoteric book—one of perhaps a thousand on his hand-hewn, rustic wooden bookshelves—and being lulled to sleep by strains of Leonard Cohen. I loved that Shane thought I was more talented than I probably actually was and how he encouraged me to write and act. I loved driving Neville to school, being the keeper of secrets he couldn't tell either of his parents. I loved how every year on Christmas Eve, Shane would dress up like Santa Claus for all the town's children and hear their wishes, and when it got really late, he'd pretend to clumsily trip up the stairs to Neville's room, waking him up to say Merry

Christmas—Neville was still unsure about the realness of Santa, when other kids had moved on long ago. ("Pull the eyebrows, that's how you know," Shane would tell him. Conveniently, both Shane and Santa were amply endowed in the eyebrow department.) What I didn't love were Shane's fits of jealousy and his angry eruptions when things didn't go according to his plan. Ironic, I know, for a former hippie cum anger-management counselor.

At work the next week after the positive pregnancy test, I slowly leaked my news about the baby, too excited to hold it in. Most people gasped with excitement, including the office manager, normally a model of etiquette and propriety. "How far along?" she gushed.

"Six weeks," I said.

She dropped her smile and said, sotto voce, "You shouldn't tell before three months." I understood that she meant, "Just in case you don't stay pregnant," but nothing bad had ever happened to my body before. Miscarriages were for other people.

Plus, I am not a secret keeper. I wanted everyone in on my joy from the beginning. We put up a poster-sized piece of paper on my office wall, and coworkers would come in and write down baby-name ideas, including the noble "Samuel" and the ridiculous "Herkermer."

My cousin Sean and his wife, Ingebjorg, gave me a soft blue blanket for the child. After several years of vegetarianism, I ate like a monster and consumed steak like it was the only substance that would keep me alive. I felt like I had unlocked a new level in the female experience: pregnant woman. I was excited to need new clothes, even to be sick. Shane and I started making plans.

Around the twelve-week mark of my pregnancy, I noticed a little blood on my underwear, and it worried me enough to go to the doctor. An ultrasound revealed there was no heartbeat. No baby. Only an empty egg sac. A hoax that made my body believe it was pregnant. It had fooled me and everyone else I brought along with me in my joy. A cruel joke that had me realize how much I wanted to be a mother.

I sobbed in the doctor's office, and there was an offer of a procedure to scrape the inside of my uterus clean, which I refused, thinking that if whatever it was, or had been, got up there just fine, it could come down on its own. I kept feeling like there was something they should have been doing to help take away the feeling of grief and helplessness—something besides making sad eyes and saying, "I'm so sorry."

My "in two years, I'll get serious about having kids" mantra had stretched into more than a decade. Once I was actually pregnant, I'd fallen madly, irreversibly in love with the idea of becoming a mom. I'd become invested in that microscopic clump of cells and what it meant. We had made life, and I had failed it.

I lay in Shane's big bed, cramping, while he was downstairs writing a play. He was sympathetic to the loss, which felt more like "mine" than "ours." I suspected he was relieved that he wouldn't have to start over again as a dad—things were good with him and Neville, two bachelor dudes living their own life. I padded my way across the hall and sat on the toilet. Suddenly, chunks of blood and biological waste the texture of slippery liver emerged from my body. I screamed. I wondered, as the seemingly endless supply coursed out of me, how it could have all built up in so short a time. I remembered a vague instruction from the doctor to try and capture the sac if I could, and I fished around with a slotted spoon to see something, anything, that resembled my baby. In that macabre stew, I found absolutely nothing that looked human.

I kept bleeding out, soaking towels. When I turned translucent white, Shane put me in the back seat of his car and drove me to the hospital. My mother, who lived across the street from the hospital, arrived and held my hand and hit the perfect motherly note for the first time I could remember.

Once, in my early twenties, Mom had prodded me to marry Nick and have children by saying, "You're not getting any younger," which I thought mean and antiwoman and absurd. But on this day, she had words of hope. "You'll try again," she said, without pressure. With only love and sadness for my loss.

My father said he would come; he lived only a half hour away. I wanted him there. I figured a hospital scenario was enough to get him up and moving. He was good at sympathy, usually, and upon the news of someone's death, he always said, "People are irreplaceable." Even if he was never a fan of my rotating cast of boyfriends—he was especially hard on Shane, whom he thought too unctuous and too old—he had warmed to the idea of me having a baby.

My dad would be my first phone call for reporting a triumph or tragedy, or if I needed a hug to muffle the world. My dad, a writer who gave me my love of words, my curiosity for others, my celebrations of the esoteric, my insatiable appetites for food and love and excellence, my sense of purpose to make the world better than I found it. But after several hours of stabilizing and doctors discussing the probability of a blood transfusion in hushed tones, I was ready to leave the hospital. Dad never made it there. I don't know why. Could it be that the sheer force of his chronic lateness beat out everything else? My best guess is that it was a pain and relief combo impossible to navigate. His daughter was miscarrying a baby from a man he didn't like or trust. During any crisis, I have found, there is one good surprise and one bad. My mom—the historically flaky parent but the one who came when I needed her—was the good surprise. My dad's nonappearance was the bad one. It's the people you think you know the best who will surprise you most, I'd find out over and over again, much to my delight and my chagrin. What I've eventually come away with, after trying unsuccessfully to train my parents to be what I thought they should be, is that the fewer expectations I have from people to give me what I need, the better. I can forage for it or it can drop on my head, but I can't demand support, love, or even the right kind of attention from anyone, especially family. If and when it comes, I'm delighted.

A couple days after the miscarriage, Shane, Neville, and I performed a small, sincere ceremony in the woods, in which I told that baby spirit to come back any time. I would be waiting.

If I was 100 percent devastated by losing the pregnancy, I was also a bonus 2 percent relieved. I had trouble imagining living out my days in Shane's drafty farmhouse. I was insensitive to Shane's art—mime—and I guess it's not cool to mime-bash your boyfriend. I also could no longer ignore his irrational cruel streak, one that I'd explained away to myself time after time. My beagle-y mutt, Lucy, my faithful familiar who slept on my bed at home and went everywhere with me, was a second-class citizen at Shane's. He would allow her to stay in the living room only, by the stove, which required her to be tied up so she wouldn't follow me upstairs. She was miserable and chewed through leash after leash. Though he'd never lay a finger on Neville, Shane was mean to his own dog, a sweet but dumb-as-a-box-of-hair Weimaraner. I was repelled by this side of Shane, but I couldn't tell you why it wasn't a deal breaker for me then, as it would be now. Sometimes you just stay. And sometimes there's an aggregate of factors, and it's a little spark that blows up the *Hindenburg*.

Six months later, as Shane and I ate dinner on my tiny Seattle patio that had a peekaboo view of Mount Rainier, I got a whiff of somebody unfamiliar to me: a smell of somebody tired, the smell of organic decay. And later that night, I saw the back label on his pants—Sansabelt. An old-man brand. My heart sunk a little deeper down into my belly. Shane and I had spent the better part of four years falling in and out of love with each other. But this was different. My attraction was waning; I was tired of being in the throes of adoration or subject to his rage—nothing in between. Shortly after the Sansabelt moment, as we were lying in bed, I ventured this: "I don't feel pretty to you anymore." I'm not sure what I was expecting. Perhaps a cross between "It's not you, it's me" and

"You are the most beautiful creature that ever set her slender, yet athletic and entirely capable foot upon the earth."

Instead, he said, "Well, you've gained weight. Physical fitness has always been more important to me than it is to you. The body of a mime, after all, is his instrument, which must be perpetually tuned."

I was quiet. My heart light fizzled out like an old tube TV turning off, fading to black.

And then we were done. For good.

I'd never thought myself overweight; I judged my body more on which clothes were fitting better. But after Shane's remark, I looked at myself differently in the mirror. My white, doughy belly. My boobs, a little sad and heavy after the miscarriage. I even found fault with my knees, which I deemed too saggy, the skin folding just so a few millimeters over the top of the kneecap.

After my initial self-pity, I joined a group of women who got their pictures taken together, naked, and then realized nobody's perfect. Bodies tell stories. I became so deeply occupied with what a few words had done to my self-esteem that I went on to create two multimedia productions about women's body-image issues called the bodyBODY Project. I rounded up a photographer and filmmaker, and I wrote plays. We embarked on an exploration about how women generally don't look like mass media suggests we should, by interviewing dozens of women about the messages they understood about their bodies and how it manifested in their everyday lives. The first show had a three-week run in a tiny Seattle theater and sold out nightly; a local college did the production as well.

Three

Hard Endings

Dad had knee-replacement surgery in December 2003 and was undergoing a ten-day recovery at the University of Washington hospital in Seattle, about a ten-minute trip from my home. He'd been a terrible prospect for the procedure, being borderline unable to undergo the surgery because of his other health complications of adult-onset diabetes and high blood pressure, but he'd bulldozed his doctors into approving the surgery, as he did whenever he didn't get his way. Afterward, the peripheral neuropathy in his feet from the diabetes coupled with the pain from his surgery made movement excruciating. He was unable to do the recovery exercises.

I took to visiting Dad in his room every other day. During one of my evening visits, we talked about my bodyBODY Project and its critical acclaim and what the next incarnation would be. He was proud of me, I could tell. He listened to my ideas about a sequel and spin-off projects, like a line of flattering, sexy clothes for bigger women. The conversation felt longer and more focused than any we'd had in recent memory. Maybe that was because he didn't have the diversions of a constantly ringing phone or piles of work from his business as the last-ditch hope for cancer patients who needed treatment resources. Maybe it was because it would be our very last conversation.

The next night, I thought about coming to see him but decided to keep on working instead. Around dinnertime, I got a call from Holly. "He's gone," she choked into the phone. I thought in all seriousness that Dad, a homebody and an impatient patient, had had enough of being in the hospital, found the keys to his Audi station wagon parked in the bowels of the hospital garage, and disappeared back to the peninsula. It took an elongated few moments for me to wrap my mind around the fact that he'd gone farther than that.

When Dad had gotten up to shuffle to the bathroom, he had dislodged a pair of blood clots from his pelvis. They had traveled to his lungs and stayed there as he squeezed out every last bit of breath from his body. Leaning on Holly, he had crumpled to the floor, calling her name three times.

I don't remember the drive to the hospital. But I do remember that when I got there, I thought that certainly there had been a mistake. That there had been some glitch and Dad was momentarily dead, but had come back. And when I saw him, big and white and still, I understood, fully, finally, how he felt when he took his own first glance at his newly deceased mother, nine years earlier. Grandmother Grace had been lying peacefully, dead, in her home hospital bed. After a harrowing forty-minute drive on windy, winding roads, which normally took an hour, Dad had burst into her room, gingerly scooped her up by the back of her neck, and kept working the muscles around her cervical spine, trying to jump-start her stagnant blood. I had finally pulled him off her, and he had wept big, salty man tears.

Now Dad was lying there, dead, in his own hospital bed, and they'd arranged some kind of wire-spring device around his face and a ball in his mouth that would let the body's gasses escape. If he were alive, he'd have thrown that damn thing across the room. Holly left me alone for a moment with Dad. I lay my body across his barrel chest, which was still warm. I settled down in a chair next to him. "Dad. Thank you. Thank you for everything you did for me. Thank you for making me and for giving me all the best parts of myself," I cried to him. And then, perhaps as a way to put a bow on a lifetime of feeling competition from a parade of girlfriends (that finally ended happily with Holly), a ghost half brother who lived a half world away, and a younger brother also vying for his attention, I said, "I'd like to think I was your favorite."

At that moment, the spring released from the device around his face and flew across the room. I took that as a yes and laugh-cried. But maybe everyone else got their own sign that they were his favorite. And I don't mind that. This one was mine.

Sometimes I dream of him. We are usually eating dinner, and I'm so happy he's come back to say hello, and sometimes there's confusion about where he really is. And I wake up with an aching missing unlike anything else I've ever felt.

By 2005, I was done with Seattle, sick of its hundred days in a row of rain and finished with its small-town claustrophobia. I was done with a dumb actor boyfriend who'd cheated on me with a married young mother from a play they were in together. (I'd seen her standing next to me at the bathroom mirror on opening night. I'd frozen for a second and said, "Break a leg," which I meant in the most literal way possible.) I was done after my second bodyBODY Project received lukewarm reviews, the product of my rushing to do whatever was next creatively without giving it time to bake properly. It was my moment for a bigger universe, somewhere I could dream bigger and do better. I thought about going back home to New York but then also recalled vowing to a resplendent Venice Beach sunset that I would return someday. I was single and free and had few ties to keep me in the Northwest, save for some beloved cousins, my aunt, and my mother. I secured a room in a Los Angeles house through Craigslist, packed all the belongings that would fit in a portable storage crate, and drove south, my dog, Lucy, riding shotgun.

In my sunny new life on Los Angeles's East Side, I was happy. Everything was fresh. I loved my newfound tribe of friends. The job I got in communications for an electric utility company offered me more than I'd ever dreamed of asking. I bought a two-bedroom apartment—a miniature version of the one I grew up in, with its wooden floors and old-timey moldings.

I scoured the Goodwill for a pair of overstuffed, shabby-chic couches and white Fiestaware dishes, and managed to find some kind of aesthetic decor harmony with the few pieces I'd inherited from my dad. Lucy the dog and I got cozy. I went on a few dates. But within a few months, I did miss the rain and the cloistered feeling of the Northwest under its great grey dome, and even the quirky folks back home.

I took a quick trip at Christmas to old, hippie Port Townsend. Ostensibly, it was to visit my mother, but there, in the parking lot of the local food co-op, I ran into Vito, an ex-boyfriend whom I'd never quite released. He was a singer: imagine Van Morrison crossed with a Connecticut-born Italian complete with an East Coast accent, who pronounces *prosciutto* "pruh-ZHUTE" and *calamari* "gala-MAR." With his light-green eyes and crazy long eyelashes set against olive skin, a flop of glossy black hair (that eventually, mostly, disappeared into a formidable buzz, the way a gracious man concedes victory to time), he'd been impossible for me to resist, again and again. We'd spent the past ten years as friends, and lovers, and people who think fondly of each other but don't get in touch. I'd leapfrogged between him and Shane a couple times. At one point, Vito and I had lived next door to each other in Seattle, sharing a common bedroom wall; he'd come to my father's funeral and cried real tears. Shane had accused me of always keeping someone in the wings, and as much as I vehemently denied it then, he was right. Vito had never been very far offstage when Shane was on, and vice versa.

But on that clear, crisp Christmas Eve day in Port Townsend, with the sun making a rare winter appearance, shining down on that little parking lot as shoppers shuttled their organic kale and gluten-free crackers to their Subarus, it turned out that dormant chemistry was still chemistry when you added a little oxygen to it. My heart stopped as we spoke, catching up on what we were doing, and I impulsively invited him to Christmas at my uncle Mike's house. He accepted, and the next day, he fell in with cousins and uncles and aunts just like old times and spent a disproportionate amount of time sprawled on the floor helping the little kids set up their toys and racetracks.

"He's auditioning," said my cousin's wife, Ingebjorg, as an aside.

Baby Game on.

That Christmas night, I stayed with Vito. He told me I was beautiful, and I felt it for the first time in many months. We rocked his antique iron bed in his farmhouse (it's not that I have a thing for men in farmhouses; it's just that there's a lot of acreage on the peninsula). I clung to him like the world would dissolve if I let go.

If you've ever been to the Olympic Peninsula in the winter, you know that there's nothing colder than a Port Townsend toilet seat, and I was reminded of this the next morning. I counted it as another reason why I'd never move back. Vito and I kept a long-distance relationship going, visiting at my place or his every few weeks. One morning, during such a visit at my place, a condom broke in the midst of sex.

We lay there quietly, the bright sun forcing its way through the curtains, lighting the room like an ad for the Sunday *New York Times*. I calculated the time from my last period and realized that we couldn't have had better timing for my fertile window if we'd tried.

"What if I am pregnant?" I asked him, half hoping he'd shrug his shoulders and let destiny take over.

His face shut down; his body tensed. "We're not ready," he said.

And I half agreed—the half that loved living on my own, the half that didn't trust we could pull off a relationship after so much back-and-forth, the half that was constantly worried about his smoking. The half that was simply afraid.

I shuffled my sorry, sad ass to the pharmacy and got Plan B, the morning-after pill to prevent pregnancy. It was like mainlining a bunch of birth-control pills. I was sickened, disheartened, hating that I'd not been 100 percent on board with the decision. I vowed I'd never change the course of a pregnancy in my body again.

We weren't ready for a child, but we were ready for more of each other. Vito started to casually look for mechanical engineering jobs in Southern California, and in a surprise to both of us, he nabbed some right off the bat. One was too far away, in Huntington Beach. One didn't pay enough. But another was perfect, right in the neighboring town. He could even ride his bike there from my place.

Without discussion of what it would be like—or even if we were going to make this a permanent arrangement—Vito drove down his old-school diesel Mercedes, packed with all his worldly goods, and moved in with me. He took over the second bedroom, which had been my office, for his private space. I moved my workstation into the dining room and the dining table into the living room, and it took a while for me to register that I had no more of my own space in my own home. Still, it was dreamy to wake up next to the man I loved every morning. We'd cook together and explore Los Angeles. We'd cheer on each other's work victories and curse idiotic bosses and colleagues. We were a team. And even though he was adamantly opposed to marriage, after his had ended painfully many years prior, we decided to have a baby together, because he loved me and it was what I wanted more than anything.

On my thirty-ninth birthday, my mother and younger brother came to stay for a few days, and my two-bedroom place suddenly felt very small. Vito and I dragged an air mattress into the vacant apartment next door. A light from the courtyard, our own personal moon, streamed through the bay windows into the otherwise dark space. It was quiet like the country, an emptiness filled with the promise of possibility. On the floor of that living room, we made a baby on the first try.

Vito took a certain pride in his virility and told everyone at his work that we were having a baby. I was not as certain, even though several positive home pregnancy tests and one trip to the doctor confirmed it. I didn't feel sick; my breasts felt disappointingly normal. It seemed a little too easy, a little too perfect.

The pregnancy was so early and small and nothing that its end, after a couple weeks, didn't even register. The ob-gyn, a Kenny Rogers look-alike with melty blue eyes, suggested progesterone and perhaps another doctor who specialized in risky pregnancies. I was furious at the gods and mad at Dr. Kenny Rogers and the nurse and receptionist for not somehow knowing it wasn't going to stick. Nobody had any words to repair me. "Just keep trying," they said.

Two months later, Vito and I went around again to create a life, and again, we got pregnant, the test said. We were quietly hopeful. As a reward for meeting sales goals, Vito's work sent the whole team and their families for a Memorial Day weekend in Santa Barbara. I declined the offer to snorkel off the Channel Islands and instead concentrated on keeping my food down and stared at the cold grey waters, hoping that nothing bad would happen to my baby's father. I drank seltzer instead of wine, hoping to protect that little life. In the hotel bathroom I took another confirmation test and peed on the plastic stick. Negative. Like nothing was ever there. Vito and I rode home on the train with his coworkers in a sad, stony silence. Nothing more to say, really.

And then we unraveled, as usual. Vito started to spend more time sitting at his computer or watching TV. We stopped having conversations. We stopped laughing. We stopped making dinners for friends. Every night I would go to bed wondering if he wanted to have sex, and every night it was apparent that he did not. We became each other's leftovers. I wanted him to be more like the Vito from ten years ago, the one who climbed rocks and sang songs around a fire.

If this had been a movie, the next scenes would be a montage: Vito watching TV after work, then me commenting on it. Without a word, him picking up the TV and putting it out on the sidewalk. Him packing up and moving out. Me following my mother's advice and throwing out all my underwear to clear my luck. Me repainting the bedroom.

Fortunately, my mother's advice worked. In the months that followed, an exotic adventure and a well-placed prayer would send me on a direct trajectory to my own motherhood.

Four

THE ASK

The first woman Dad married was Liz, a pianist who'd achieved a modicum of success. Their union was fraught with turmoil and fear—I will never really know the absolute truth, but I'm certain it's somewhere in the very murky, problematic spectrum between what she said ("He was angry and abusive") and what he told me ("I never hit her, but I did defend myself when she attacked me"). To bulletproof her escape from my father, Liz, who is Jewish, moved to Israel when their son, my half brother, Ilya, was only three, in 1968. There was no way Dad, a strapping Irish Catholic who had been marked as a violent man, could make a case to see his first child, despite repeated pleas to all governments involved. In desperation, he once traveled to Israel and poorly executed a snatch-back scheme to take Ilya from the yard at his kindergarten. Ilya, who had been groomed to be perpetually on the lookout for his monster father, screamed, and the plan failed. There was one heavily supervised visit in Israel allowed when Ilya was about ten.

When Dad died, I found file cabinets packed full of paperwork and legal correspondence pleading to see Ilya that spanned all of the 1970s and went into the 1980s, physical manifestations of Dad's broken heart. During my childhood, Ilya was our shadow sibling—the one who was not as lucky as my younger brother and I were, the one who was being kept by his mother from seeing his own dad. Because we'd only heard about him, he was an abstract, a cause, a permanent scar nobody could see but we could all feel.

The first time I met Ilya in person was when I was sixteen and he was nineteen. He arrived at my dad's home in Port Ludlow, Washington, on the Olympic Peninsula. We spent a good deal of time just marveling at each other, trying to decode the genetic similarities. He looked so much like a younger version of my dad, with the same square Irish jaw, strong nose, and eyes, which felt uncanny and perfect at the same time. But I thought him odd, too, unlike anyone I'd ever met. He didn't ever edit his thoughts and just said whatever was on his mind, like that he found all women in our community too fat. During his visit, he jogged fifteen miles of country roads to visit us at school and hung out with me for the day. I felt as close to him as if we'd fought over the last of the cereal and created pillow forts together our whole lives.

I hung out with Ilya in the States through the years, mostly in New York, when he came to visit his mother and stepfather after they moved into a former Brooklyn brothel they'd scored in a great deal. They kept a house in Tel Aviv for vacations, because it was easier for them to live in the States and because of Israel's ongoing tumultuous political climate. But I'd never visited Ilya in Israel, which he considers his home. In 2008, he was engaged to marry a beautiful, creative, warm woman named Sigal, whom everyone calls Gali. She'd just given birth to their baby boy, Adam. They wanted me there for the ceremony, and I felt up to the adventure. Without thinking too hard about it, I booked a ticket.

Getting onto the Jerusalem-bound flight from Heathrow was the most difficult part of the trip. A slight delay in my first flight's arrival made me run for the gate, and I got there with zero moments to spare. El Al airline agents took my bag and methodically unpacked every single item in it, while a full plane of passengers waited for us.

"What's this?" they asked.

"A flat iron?" I responded, unsure if there was some trick answer I was supposed to know. "For my hair?"

"Have you been to Israel before?"

"No, this is my first time."

"What is the purpose of your trip?"

"I'm visiting my brother."

"Why does your brother live there?"

"His mother brought him there when he was three." This was getting complicated. But I thought it best to omit any reference to kidnapping from my narrative.

And on it went, until the agents were somehow convinced I was not a terrorist, just a bumbling little fool with a complex family situation who couldn't quite describe why she wasn't an actual Jew but was visiting her Jewish brother in Israel anyway.

I'm not religious, but I like to say I'm Jew-*ish*. My parents were brought up Catholic, but my father took Yiddish at Yale because of his love of languages (he was fluent in French and could get by in Spanish, Italian, German, and Russian) and his attraction for Jewish culture. Speaking Yiddish would also give him an in with pretty Jewish girls, he thought.

For my eleventh summer, my father signed me up for catechism at the Holy Trinity School around the block. This was partly to give me a religious foundation, but mostly to get me out of the house. There I sat in a 1929 brick building, blond wooden floors worn smooth by generations of kids, the only white face amid the Haitian students, who had arrived in the neighborhood as first-generation refugees with their parents. This wasn't anything new; I'd been in a bilingual program with mostly Haitians for the first four years of my schooling, but they'd not yet quite gotten the hang of the immersion teaching. The few native English-speaking kids could barely converse in French; the Haitian kids fared much better because they were in New York and had English all around them. My catechism class was in French, and I caught about every fourth word. I tried to understand the Father–Son–Holy Ghost connection—how could they be one and, at the same time, three separate entities? And if I was God's child, Jesus seemed superfluous. But I couldn't communicate my confusion to the teacher. Or anyone else. So I decided at a very young age that religion was a collection of artfully told, made-up stories. There were so many versions. Nobody could possibly have the truth.

I'd always felt a very tenuous connection, at best, between religion and spirituality. On paper, I'm baptized Greek Orthodox—the Catholics wouldn't allow a baptism because my father hadn't annulled his marriage to Ilya's mother. My mother, Catholic turned hippie turned Buddhist turned wholistic "God Is Good," made nature her main religion, and in the mid-1970s, after she and my father divorced, Mom started the Central Park Historical Society with her boyfriend. They would show people around the entire park on weekend mornings for a few bucks a head; I could lead the entire tour by the time I was eleven, and I inherited her adoration and respect for the grand designs and tiny miracles of the earth. Mom had shopped us around at different Sunday schools, and the one I remember the most was the Christian Science class (which I still find very useful for car repair and also for letting things go until absolutely medically necessary). I had always considered myself connected to God, though, in some way, using mediums such as Buddhist chants or nature or coincidences to better understand her/him/it. To me, Jesus seemed more of a kindly middleman and historical teacher, a hero in a story like so many others—Odysseus, Moses, Superman.

I've never felt like I belong to any one religion, nor have I felt like any religion wanted me enough to claim me.

Which brings me to the spring of 2008, when Israel was scrubby with green patches surrounded by endless topaz waters. Israel was my hair misbehaving very, very badly and me never quite getting the salt off from floating in the Dead Sea. Israel was magic and complicated, and I felt the mysticism and beauty under every pebble. Ilya and Gali lived way out in the country, about halfway between Tel Aviv and Jerusalem, in a village called Tzafririm, which Ilya said roughly translates to "Morning Devils."

The first few days, Ilya, Gali, and I sat around the table and Monday-morning quarterbacked the last forty-two years. Our versions of history clashed. Accusations became memories that had become truths. I felt defensive of my father—I'd experienced his fury, but I didn't think he could be violent, as Liz had asserted. I have since learned that women rarely lie about this, though, and also, when I asked my mother if he was violent with her, she indicated that yes, he was. Ilya and I kept reminding each other and ourselves that the past, while not irrelevant, didn't need to be figured out, because we were good, we were here, we were family.

One morning, we piled into Ilya's tiny, beat-up pickup and drove out to where the roads became rutted paths, which led us to a sea of a few hundred goats. The Bedouins who were chasing them stopped for a moment and invited us to drink tea made of sage and sugar under their tarp tents. Ilya and Gali spoke to them in Arabic. Four or five children ran around, shy and smiling. The little boys threw clumps of grass and mud at a donkey to make him bray, which was hilarious for everyone except the donkey.

Toward the end of the week, we made the two-plus-hour trek to Tel Aviv for the wedding, held in the town house Ilya's mother and stepfather (whom he actually called dad) owned, just a few short blocks from the azure Mediterranean Sea. I went with the betrothed as they made their rounds prepping for the party and getting fitted with wedding clothes—Ilya, Gali, and the baby all wore some version of a light, shimmery linen. The night before, Gali and her girlfriends and mother and I sat on the floor sewing small charms onto her chuppah, a traditional wedding canopy. Finally, on the wedding day, friends helped string the rooftops with party lights and people arrived, cheerful, dressed in dazzling colors, in clothes made for dancing. I was introduced as Ilya's sister, though he had other, younger ones, which caused polite, initial puzzlement until Ilya or Gali explained in Hebrew. One of Ilya's oldest friends, Amir, was there, and we remembered each other from gallivanting around New York. Guests talked to "the American sister" in English both halting and perfect. I never once felt out of place or like a stranger. We danced and laughed and ate way into the night, twirling close to the edge of the roof, overlooking the twinkling water. It felt like home, a different dimension of family than what I was used to.

We beat it out of gritty, hot, complicated Tel Aviv a day or two later and arrived at the Dead Sea to stay with Ilya's friend at a nearby kibbutz. When we woke, early, we four-wheeled it to the shore (think rocky, desert lunar scape), soaked in hot springs, slapped mud all over ourselves, and floated in the body-temperature water that brims with so much salt that nothing can stay alive in it, yet everything can stay up. Ilya knows nothing about body modesty—he comes from a line of men who leave their junk hanging out, putting the onus on their company to avert their eyes, or not. Once, he was leading a group of German tourists through the Sinai desert. They'd not seen anyone else for days. He convinced them to hike naked, and once they disrobed, of course that was when other people crossed their path.

Now, here in the Dead Sea, everyone else stripped down to float without a thought, and I followed form, shoving aside my Americanness.

As I lay at the water's edge, my torso in the stream of super-salty, hot water rushing from the pool and my legs out toward the cooler seawater, it felt that there had to be a general sin cleansing with all this washing over of salt and water and history. How could there not be?

On the way back to Ilya's home, we stopped at a gas station where you could buy dates and take a ride on Shi-Shi the camel, who was waiting, his caramel-colored fur collecting desert dust, his wide mouth stretched into a sort of perma-smile across his face. Ilya had some words with the attendant, and moments later they hoisted me up atop Shi-Shi, who trotted a little too quickly for my comfort as the sun set its blazing red self behind the horizon.

We went to Jerusalem for one of the last days of my visit. I wanted to inhale the ancient city, thick with history and color and spices. I took hundreds of pictures in the old market, where I meandered through stalls selling chess sets; spices arranged into precise, immaculate towers (ten years later, I still have some saffron that I use, pinch by tiny pinch); and charms to ward off the evil eye.

Ilya and Gali needed to deliver a suitcase to a friend of a friend, a nun named Sue, at the Russian Orthodox Convent of Saint Mary Magdalene. We drove up a steep hill toward the church's gleaming golden domes, one of the highest points in the city. I felt a little sad that I was not of this denomination, that I didn't have the faith that the religious tourists did. Sue, originally from California, had become a nun after being miraculously cured from cancer by drinking goat milk; her cell phone kept going off with "Ave Maria" as the ringtone. I loved her instantly.

At the church, a docent led us on a tour and lectured in English about the ocher-red Russian Orthodox Easter eggs lovingly depicted on the walls: the color symbolizes the blood of Christ; the shell, the impenetrable tomb from which he emerged. I wandered around and admired the art, the fine craftwork, and the ornate devotion of the believers.

At some point I found myself alone, outside in the church's small cemetery, on a scrubby patch of grass, high above the city. I looked down over Jerusalem, a jumble of bricks and people and donkeys and shopping and layers of history too old and complicated for my little American mind to comprehend. And then there was a voice. Not a voice of anyone I knew. It was not male or female, or high or low. But I heard it, clearly, as if someone next to me were speaking.

The voice said: "It's OK to ask for miracles."

There was nobody next to me, nobody around me. But I know it happened from outside me. I double-checked. Nope. Nobody there. It felt like the opportunity of a lifetime—as if I had won a million-dollar sweepstakes but had to make a speech in order to claim it.

My brain reached around the concept of a miracle. What did I want most that was the most unlikely thing to occur? Make it good, I told myself. This is your chance.

It hadn't occurred to me to ask for any miracles, ever. In fact, I'm usually a little afraid to pray because I don't want to use up too many favors. What if there's a fire or a similarly urgent situation that takes up more prayer karma than I have left? What if God is busy and doesn't get the message, and it just doesn't happen? What would that mean for my ambiguous faith if my prayers failed to manifest?

But it seemed that I had been given permission from someone, somewhere, and I wasn't going to analyze it too much for fear that I'd talk myself out of it. I'd tried so hard and failed so many times to make a relationship that led to marriage that led to a baby—even skipping straight to making the baby. I was out of plans and out of answers and out of options.

And suddenly it was OK to ask for miracles.

So I asked, quietly.

"I would like someone to love me enough to have a child with me. Please."

I half expected something significant to happen, but the ground didn't move. There was no clap of thunder or sudden surge of swallows. Not even a rustle of the breeze or the dropping of a leaf. But, for no outward or logical reason, I did feel an inner knowing that my order had been received, stamped, and was on its way to processing.

PART II

Everything You've Ever Been or Said or Done in Your Whole Life Has Led Up to This Very Second

Five

WHEN YOU KNOW WHERE YOU WANT TO GO BUT CAN'T FIGURE OUT HOW TO GET THERE

A few days after I returned home to Los Angeles from the Israel miracle-asking trip, I was wandering through Cost Plus World Market, an import store. I'd been churning over my parenting options, with the understanding that my prayer could help but I'd have to do a lot of the heavy lifting. The Kenny Rogers gyno had uttered "high-risk pregnancy" after the last miscarriage with Vito, my third and final pregnancy. I had about a 25 percent chance of conceiving without medical intervention, and that number was dipping lower every month.

I moved along the kitchenware section, contemplating a long, thin white ceramic dish created especially for the service of olives. How often did I actually serve olives? Should I be the kind of person who had a dedicated dish for olives? As a kind of mini moving meditation, I traced my fingers along the ethnically inspired curtains hanging in a row. Easter loomed. Imported Belgian chocolate eggs, anyone? (Who was I kidding? I'd eat them all myself.)

High risk. Like I didn't work right. My body was a threat to itself. At thirty-nine. How could that possibly be old? I didn't feel old. I didn't look old. The thought that I might not be able to make a baby wasn't so much of a slow dawning, more of a plop and thud, a rock into my brainpan. This was going to be harder than I thought.

I didn't have a husband or boyfriend or a friend with benefits or even a lovely gay best friend who would be up for the deed. How would I even start?

And then, somewhere in the neighborhood of a carved teak room divider and an ikat-print table runner, I saw Bunny. She was a soft, stuffed powder-pink Easter toy with an ostrich-egg-shaped face; little, beady black eyes; and a small, stitched smile under her nose. I picked up Bunny and put her down. If I were a kid, I'd like this bunny, I thought. I was always more of a stuffed-animal lover than a Barbie person. My wish still felt so incomplete and sketchy, along the lines of throwing a coin into an ocean instead of a fountain. Vague hope.

I'd been paying attention to how other people made families, even people I didn't know very well. I'd met a woman from New York at a conference who had also come to this point—she was an accomplished professional with her own PR agency, who'd made it to her late thirties with no prospects for her baby's daddy. She took a withdrawal from a sperm bank. And just like that, she gave birth to a ginger-haired boy she named Sascha, who looked exactly like her.

I imagined scrolling through sperm-donor profiles. I guess I'd pick someone who had facility with language and music. Someone on the tall side. Probably with my coloring so that there wouldn't be too many awkward questions about paternity. The thought of choosing a father had a certain appeal, but the idea of sitting legs up in the gyno's office to be inseminated and the subsequent anxiety about the pregnancy sticking sounded like an outer circle of fertility hell. It wasn't for me. What if I needed IVF or another complicated and painful procedure to get pregnant? I'd known others who had gone before. Some succeeded, some failed. I was spooked.

I imagined my savings draining away and being broke, baby-less, and bitter at the end of it.

The only other route was adoption. I wasn't close with anyone who'd adopted, but I knew that you had to look good on paper, which I did: a job with benefits and a steady income, I was a property owner, without a criminal record or even a speeding ticket in the past decade. I was a nice person who did well in interviews. How hard could it be? Yes, adoption, probably.

I knew that little baby spirit was out there. It didn't matter if she came to me through my body, was left on my doorstep, or was handed to me by a stranger. If it took adoption for us to find each other, so be it.

I picked up that pink bunny in Cost Plus and purchased her as a talisman, a marker, a lucky charm. Bunny lived patiently on the futon for two years until a child—my child—finally clutched her in her chubby arms, sighing sleeping baby breaths into her face.

~

Up through the 1990s, my career had included stints as a waitress and bartender. I'd owned a dating service in a small town and edited books from a niche, controversial, libertarian-leaning publisher that taught people how to live under fake IDs and avoid paying taxes. The main through line, though, was that all of it happened to support what I really loved the most: being a journalist like my dad and his dad before him.

I'd been on staff at magazines and newspapers since that first job at that tiny New Mexico newspaper and alternated those stints with long periods of freelancing, writing travel and business stories. To this day, I get a buzz when I think of a good article, then subsequent hits when I sell it, finish writing it, and see it in print (or in "print" online). It is the job I feel best about doing, especially because I get to write stories about feminist parenting and money, and sometimes the intersection of both. Now, I also write for banks and big brands that offer better-paying, more consistent work.

In 2006, a year after moving to Southern California and before I went on the trip to Israel, I'd landed a full-time job. The freelance-writing universe was becoming upended as digital media sucker punched the traditional kind. I was new to the area and wasn't confident enough to pitch travel stories from an unfamiliar place. I thought, I'll do this for six months until I get my footing, but that six months stretched into seven years at the first company, and a year at another. Every weekday, I'd get up, put on some corporate clothing combo of "nice" pants or a pencil skirt, heels, and a blazer, a walking homage to discount retailers' misses career separates sections. My first job entailed creating content for an electric utility whose parent company sat squarely in the Fortune 200 list. It was a very buttoned-up, "we've always done things this way" kind of place, and my friends wondered how I—somewhat irreverent and impatient—would ever make it in that world. But during my first few days at work, my kind, funny boss, John, handed me a book called *Orbiting the Giant Hairball: A Corporate Fool's Guide to Surviving with Grace*, about a creative type making it in a business situation, and for that he forever earned my undying loyalty and best ideas. He saw me; he got me.

I'd always wanted to find meaning in my work and wondered if that was possible now that I'd moved into something so radically different than anything I'd ever done. But John showed me the secret ways for people like me to navigate corporate America, which mostly involved playing micro political games and doing some PowerPoint presentations about how whatever unorthodox strategy I had would improve the company's bottom line and make shareholders happy. I loved working on renewable energy and efficiency initiatives. I made more cash than I'd ever dreamed of when I was scraping by as a freelance magazine writer, and I rode out the recession with a steady paycheck.

Our executives had just signed a contract for the largest solar deal in the United States. I'd meticulously planned a PR campaign and cultivated a list of renewable energy and sustainability bloggers, in addition to high-level journalists from the *New York Times* and other news sources of national renown. I sat in my grey upholstered cubicle, fielding call after call, doing a kind of mental victory dance when each new news item popped up in my inbox. At the end of the day, John called me into his office. I slumped down in the chair, wrung out with a happy exhaustion.

"I imagine you're ready to take a victory lap right about now," he said, noting the information I'd pushed out had landed on Google's front news page.

There have been a handful of moments in my career when I felt truly, unstoppably proud of my work, and this was one of them.

After a couple years I got in my professional groove, becoming an expert at corporate communications. I was surprised that I liked it. And most surprising of all, sometimes in corporate America you find your spouse.

My miracle-asking episode in Israel was a couple weeks behind me, and I was getting back into the swing of normalcy: answering emails, talking to the press about our environmental initiatives, attending the endless stream of coworker baby and wedding showers. One day I was invited to a meeting in a building where I never went, in a window-less room that reminded me of a public school's storage area, with its painted cinder-block walls and a table that took up nearly the entire space. Going in, I remarked out loud, to nobody in particular, "This is not my beautiful house." And I caught the ear of someone, who turned around to look at me and smile. He was tan, a little weatherworn, with eyes the blue color of a wave just before it breaks. Tall. Ruddy. The exact thought I had when I saw him was this: He's the kind of guy who comes home after a day of sailing to a couple gin and tonics. I don't know where I got the sailing part from. He just had a weathering in a way that only the sea can bring.

We all went around the room introducing ourselves, and I realized Tan Guy, who introduced himself as Peter, was indeed *that* Peter, the one I'd been calling for a couple years with the occasional data requests. He'd always been professional, polite, and had a resonant, irresistible FM deejay voice. I knew nothing about him personally, but as I looked at him across the table—that competent, cool demeanor, the go-to man for major problems—he seemed solid and sure. So solid, in fact, he'd worked in the same job for twenty-five-plus years. We chatted on the way out of the meeting. I noticed he was not wearing a wedding ring.

We started to exchange pleasant, work-adjacent emails, and in one of them, he invited me, along with a group of other coworkers, to hear his band play. I drove the ninety minutes south from home to Dana Point, near the ocean, where he'd set up with another dude with a guitar, so it wasn't quite a band. Neither was it exactly a show, just them at a nearly empty Starbucks, where his nephew worked, spiking Frappuccinos with whiskey and sliding them to Peter and his friend. As it was Saint Patrick's Day, they sang songs of dubious Irish origin—"I Would Walk 500 Miles" was fun but not exactly Irish.

After three songs, they were ready to pack it in.

"I didn't come all the way down here just for three songs," I said, rather bummed that the time I'd spent listening to "the band" was only a fraction of the travel time to get there and back. His friend left, the shop was closing, and we were alone. "Let's go for a drink," I suggested.

At a nearby restaurant, warmed by the orange glow of propane heaters, we settled at a patio table. It felt like a date.

He told me about his days as a rock star in Southern California, managed by Barry Manilow's partner, Garry Kief. We talked about people from work. All the while, I tried on scenarios in my mind. What if we liked each other after this? How attracted was I, exactly? Would we have to sneak around at work if we started dating?

About forty-five minutes in, the chemistry felt thicker as we started telling stories about our personal lives, veering into "so, are you dating anyone?" territory.

"I have to tell you something. I'm in a loveless marriage," he said in a way that made me think he just didn't want to admit it but felt like he had to. "We've been together for seventeen years. One of us sleeps on the couch every night—whoever gets to bed last."

It seemed like we'd talked a little too long before he'd dropped that.

"Huh, OK," I said, and didn't press him too hard about the troubles in his relationship.

Immediately, I relegated him to the Friend Zone, but it still struck me as so odd that he'd wait that long to tell me this critical piece of news, and even odder still that if he was in a bad marriage, why they were living together.

Still, at work Peter would send me flirty emails, and we corresponded throughout the day over our company's instant messaging. I learned that he had two teenage daughters and that his son was grown and was about to become a dad. He told me his wife had asked for a divorce, but neither of them had taken the first step to make it happen. In fact, all the husbands and wives resented each other in the cul-de-sac where they lived, and every night the men congregated and drank beer in the garage of one guy they called the Pool Man. I felt sorry for Peter, this sweet and solid and simple man with a rock 'n' roll edge. How could someone be so unloved in his own home?

Because we were friends, I took him to dinner for his birthday.

We sat at a white-clothed table in a seafood restaurant in the beach town where he'd grown up, the same place where he'd worked decades ago as a line cook. I picked at my salmon, he at his halibut. The wine went down easily enough. Friends, though, I kept thinking. We're going to be great friends.

After the complimentary ice cream with a candle, the evening still felt young. We slipped into a bar down the block and shot pool.

And finally, when it was too late to make excuses for staying later, we left. We walked to his truck and started kissing in the wide front seat, fogging up the windows, the waves crashing quietly in the distance.

We began to talk on the phone at night and text each other. "When are you going to tell your family about me?" I asked. "I don't want this to feel like an affair."

I just figured, hey, they had kids and a house. It was complicated. But we were all honest, levelheaded adults. Right?

"I'll tell them when it's time," Peter said.

That time didn't come. His wife, Kate, "looking for her lip gloss" in his truck, came upon a flirty email to me he'd printed out because it had directions to a restaurant in it.

Whatever tiny, miniscule amount of love may have been left in their marriage was overwhelmed by a mad, feverous rage.

Kate, her heart on fire, started to send me emails, vacillating between accusing me of stealing Peter and telling me I could have her old, good-for-nothing husband, to please take him off her hands.

Her wrath threw me off balance—I hadn't expected it, after Peter's description of their relationship. There was that foundation of seventeen years and a house and two kids and renovating and "should we put this table here," but the emotional glue that kept it all together had thinned. She was furious—and why wouldn't she be? She was a real estate agent who made nearly nothing; her pillar of support from a man with a steady job who had been, until this point, entirely trustworthy, crumbled seemingly overnight. She'd have to figure out work and money and how to parent two teen girls without a husband around. But also, I thought she must be mistaken. He was a gem but slept on the couch. What kind of fool would pass up such a loving, sweet guy? Obviously, the divorce was her fault!

He was, clearly, so loving. "Why would she throw a good man away?" he'd asked me in the dark, in my bed. I had no idea, but her trash was my treasure, I thought.

Peter's divorce became a recurring theme in our relationship, and I was starving for daily details as they inched closer to their legal split, only to rebound to square one when they couldn't agree on something. By 2009 the Southern California housing market had slipped perilously low, and Kate skillfully negotiated to sell their home for exactly what they owed. Peter, who paid most of his six-figure salary to Kate for alimony and child support and another chunk to pay down their debt, moved into his brother's suburban condo, taking a dumpy little room with a twin bed.

I'd fancied myself a cool stepmom figure and was excited by the prospect of hanging out with two young women, hearing their music, helping them get a toehold on their dreams. I imagined us shopping and cooking, sharing secrets and creating a complex system of inside jokes and references.

It didn't take long for me to realize that whatever hopes I'd had for the stepkid relationship, the entry point was all wrong. They had no interest in friending me, the woman who'd apparently busted up their nuclear family, who'd sent them to an apartment from their sprawling suburban home, who'd stolen their dad. They were angry at Peter and, for the first few weekends of the split, would begrudgingly visit him in his new place, jamming into the small room he had for them, painted cotton-candy pink. And soon after, it became painfully obvious that they didn't want to be at Peter's. There was never anything fun to do, and they stopped coming.

Peter's parents, on the other hand, made better in-laws than I could have ever invented from my imagination. They'd been warm and welcoming to me from the beginning, despite the messy divorce.

Christmas, Easter, and Thanksgiving would look like this: Peter and I would drive to their house, a sweet ranch home with a pool and patio, lovingly decorated by his mother over the past forty-odd years. His dad, a retired sheriff's deputy, would regale us with stories of how he chased down elusive arsonists and the time he had to go to New York to extradite a suspect and had a weekend to kill, so he saw the Rockettes. I'd try to be helpful in the kitchen. The girls sat glumly, speaking only when spoken to, occupied by their phones through most everything. The star of the show was Peter's baby grandson from his older son, all big blue eyes and smiles, and everyone would just watch his every move and ooh and aah, and it would take the pressure off having to endure an awkward conversation.

The only major problem with Peter as a boyfriend, though—besides that he had a not-quite-ex-wife, and he was handling that—was that he was no longer able to have biological children and had no plans to address that.

"There are ten reasons I can think of, off the top of my head, why you shouldn't date me," I'd told him during one of our early outings, at a neighborhood restaurant over a plate of steak. "The first is that I'm not very good at relationships. Everything always seems to implode, and I don't want to marry the people who want to marry me, and vice versa. The second is that I want a child. That's not going to change. And that has to happen pretty soon."

"I'm not scared," Peter said. He seemed fine with all of it. He was in. I had a pretty good feeling he was my miracle. I wasn't sure how we were going to become parents together, but I was pretty certain we were, somehow.

Six

Everyone Alive Is in a Modern Family

I was closing in on forty-one. My clock was ticking on high. I'd see pregnant women walking down the street, and I'd long to shop for maternity clothes, wondering about the day I could no longer fit into even my oldest, most stretched-out yoga pants. I also had a reservoir of baby love simmering inside me, about to burst from my chest, nowhere to go. My Baby Game had throttled up to full-fevered frenzy; all my chips were on Peter to come through as a dad, as he had three times before with two other women.

I understood Peter's girls were navigating their own ocean of emotions, and I desperately tried to connect. I shopped for them. Tried to be complimentary, tried to be cool. Sometimes I felt like we connected. But most times, we didn't. Positioning myself as stepmother was more nerve-racking than fulfilling, even though I'd confidently thought I could handle any parenting situation, given my own background of divorce and new people coming and going in and out of my parents' lives. I had chops! I had insight! I had no idea what I was doing, really. You can't make people love you. Either they do or they don't.

If I had my own baby, I could love her and she would love me back, on our own terms. We'd make our life as a complete family.

Meanwhile, the stress of Peter's divorce was starting to wear us raw. We'd do things like coupled people do—have holidays, go to dinner, and take the odd weekend away. It had also dawned upon me, slowly, that when we were both drinking, we'd get into some emotional tussle and then I'd always have to say that one extra thing, the last lethal word that would result in a prolonged, stormy silence until the negative energy dissipated. We had our worst fight when we were on a vacation in the Turks and Caicos that I'd won on a game show.

Sometimes you drink with someone because it's more fun that way. You get silly and confessional. You think you're relating more deeply. It was like this, for me, with Peter. But drinking was also a pitchfork that would stab through any bubble of happiness we'd created. On that night on vacation, we'd been out for dinner and had a few cocktails after, and in bed, we were talking about Peter's daughters. "I wish they weren't being so horrible," I said, a result of my hurt feelings from their campaign to ostracize us from their lives when all we wanted was to bring everyone together. I thought he'd agree, but he was silent and rightly so. He didn't want to hear any judgment around his kids. Had I been sober, I wouldn't have said anything at all—or maybe I would have approached it with more kindness. Peter reached over and turned the light out. In the sad silence the mosquito netting swayed softly from the breeze of the ceiling fan. Drinking is fun until it isn't.

It was impossible to plan any kind of future, as Peter's finances were tied up supporting his other family, and the complex negotiations around their split seemed to continually put the end zone farther and farther down the field. We would break up and make up several times from the stress of his divorce.

Once, while we were broken up, we both decided we'd still show up at a Hollywood open-mic night run by friends. He got up on stage with his guitar. I nursed a glass of wine. And then he belted out, in that sexy baritone, Barry Manilow's "Could It Be Magic." He knew that was my emotional Achilles' heel, and he'd doubled down on the impact by changing the name of the song's subject from *Melissa* to *Vanessa*.

I'd been to see Barry Manilow in Las Vegas a few months before, for my fortieth birthday. I'd been obsessed with him since my friend Lisa and I were eight or nine. We'd lie on her brother's bed, playing both sides of *Tryin' to Get the Feeling* and *Barry Manilow II* on vinyl over and over again.

That Peter took the trouble to learn the song and show up to play it was the ultimate salve for my ego, a slam dunk of a romantic gesture. He also wrote a long, loving email to me, declaring he was "all in," and we got back together. He didn't have anything going on in his life that would eclipse becoming a father again. And for me, perhaps the journey would go faster if we traveled together. I knew he'd be a good dad.

In the five months we were apart, I'd been busy. I'd made calls to friends of friends who were adoptive parents, to get the lowdown. The sister of a close friend told me that she'd taken in a baby boy from the foster system and was almost ready to finalize the adoption after a year, and then the father's family swooped in and reclaimed him. Choosing an agency turned out to be a modern Goldilocks exercise: one agency outright refused me because I was not married. Another private attorney would cost $80,000, much more than I had to spend. I kept researching online and sending away for brochures. One from the Kinship Center, a nonprofit, arrived in the mail, and I glanced at the orientation meeting date—it was the next night. I decided to go; it was a tiny action that would inch me closer to becoming a mom.

We were about a year into our rocky courtship, and Peter's divorce was still dragging on. One night we sat on my couch, in the middle of our James Bond marathon—our goal was to watch every single one. (Best Bond? Connery, Moore, and Craig and Brosnan tied for third, in that order, for me.) There was a knock on the door, and I opened it to see my neighbor Maddie, a twentysomething single mom of two boys, who'd started having children early, when she was fifteen. A rich kid from school was the dad of the first child; her high school teacher was the father of the second. Both boys lived mostly with their dads, as Maddie worked long hours as an HR professional. She'd just started dating a very cute French swimmer, Alain.

"Can I come in? I need to ask you something."

She came in, just to the door, and didn't sit down.

"I'm pregnant."

"Wow! Congrats?"

I wasn't sure if this was good or bad news for her.

"I know you're adopting a baby. Do you think you'd want this one? Alain and I just aren't ready yet."

I held my breath as she explained, a slow-motion moment. This could be it. I carefully, cautiously unfolded the hope I always kept tucked away inside me.

We were friends. She was so funny and bright and fearless, her arms amassing a collection of highly personal, deeply artistic tattoos. She'd shown up at midnight on my fortieth birthday and handed me a lovely gift of bangle bracelets; I'd brought her to one of Peter's gigs, moving our friendship beyond the porch we shared. But she also had a volatile family life—her father, whom she didn't know growing up, lived in Tokyo and hit on her when they finally met in person when she was an adult. Her mother was always plagued by money troubles, once leaving Maddie alone for months to care for her younger brothers when she was a young teen. Maddie went to work as an escort to pay the rent. I wasn't sure why she asked me, but maybe it just seemed like the perfect situation. She wasn't ready. I was.

"We're not asking anyone else. I think you'd be an amazing mom," she said, fiddling with the fastener on her overalls.

I leaned toward yes, even though I wondered about logistics. Would they stay next door? Would that be weird? Would they babysit? What would the kid think? We told Maddie we'd discuss it.

I closed the door, wide-eyed, dumbfounded, and looked at Peter. My dog, Lucy, used to chase squirrels with the vehemence of a cheetah going for a gazelle after a long fast. She'd spent her life shooting off after them, only to lose them when they'd invariably scoot up a tree she couldn't climb, though she tried. But there was one time she actually caught a squirrel by the tail. She stopped and froze and looked at me. She wasn't quite sure what to do at that moment, once she'd gotten what she wanted. I felt a little like Lucy at this moment.

Peter and I sat back on the couch.

"I don't think so. I'm not ready. I'm not even divorced," he said.

His divorce was still trudging through legal sludge. I couldn't argue because he was right. And living next to the birth parents? It would have been messy and weird and awkward and something very deep inside me knew it was not the right situation.

I wondered how in the ever-loving hell to say no to what I wanted most in the entire world. I wanted this with or without Peter, but I happened to be with him, so I couldn't just steamroll such a major life move. The decision process felt surreal, like I was watching myself in a movie or reading about a woman in a book. I felt a flash of hatred for Peter and loathed the safeness of it all. That his decision would tip fate in an unpredictable way.

I sat at my desk and held my breath, and sent an email to Maddie. "I am honored you've thought of us, but it is too soon in our relationship to bring a child in."

A few days later, Maddie knocked on the door. She leaned in, past the screen, and I hoped she was going to tell me they'd found a good family or that they'd decided to go ahead and keep the baby. "I just wanted to tell you I got an abortion," she said. She'd tell Alain, who later became her husband and, later, ex-husband, that she'd miscarried. A hug, a few words of grief and sorrow, and I closed the door gently behind her.

I made my way to the bathroom, the universal default hub for women who can't hold it together. I hunched over the tub, slipping to the cold tile floor as a kind of spiritual flogging. Sobs lurched from the deepest place inside me, racking my body. What had I done? I was a monster. I'm pro-choice. I've volunteered for a pro-choice organization and have disgust and disdain for any kind of rule that jeopardizes a woman's decisions. But in that instant, I felt like that little clump of cells, given a chance, could have been my child. I promised I would never, ever say no again when given such an opportunity. Peter watched all this, unsure what to do in the face of my emotional hurricane. He couldn't help. I knew he wanted to, but he couldn't. Nobody could. Even my dog, Lucy, had let that squirrel go, standing forlorn and still, watching it scamper away.

Maddie became a mom again, a year or so later, to a beautiful baby girl. I was happy for them and couldn't help wondering, sometimes, about what would have happened if she'd made another choice and offered the baby to us again. And what if we'd made another choice and said yes. But it's sort of worthless to think about such things, because that leads to regrets and resentments.

On my forty-second birthday, five weeks after his divorce was final, Peter invited two of my best girlfriends to dinner at our house. He grilled a fine piece of halibut and served it with sweet mango relish on top—to this day, probably the nicest piece of fish I've ever had. Another friend baked and delivered a German chocolate cake, her annual tradition for my birthday. Then Peter instructed me to walk over to my computer and put a disc in. A movie came up, him playing "Happy Birthday" on his guitar. At the end of the song, Movie Peter said, "Turn around." And there he was in real life on one knee, with a ring box opened to reveal a white-gold ring with tiny diamonds and a zinfandel-colored morganite stone in the center. We'd picked it out a few weeks before. "Will you do me the honor of becoming my wife?" he asked.

For what seemed like a very, very long two seconds, I regretted that he'd asked in front of witnesses. I'd always been embarrassed by other people's JumboTron stadium proposals and the ones in restaurants where the ring is presented in the dollop of whipped cream atop the chocolate lava cake and everyone else claps.

"Yes," I said, despite mild mortification, and slipped the ring on. We were happy. We popped sparkling wine, and the next morning I left for a ten-day work junket to Japan. I stared at my sparkly ring during the entire trip.

We stripped my second bedroom of its dowdy antique pink-and-gold wallpaper and painted it cotton white with a gender-neutral spring-green trim, splattering paint, being happy in the mess, just like a couple in a home-improvement-store commercial. I picked up an irresistible yellow Paul Frank baby hoodie with a monkey face and hung it in the closet. That and the pink bunny were the only two items I allowed myself to buy for the baby: they signified hope; they marked a place. Too many things would seem like a weight on my expectation. Like a prayer shouted, not whispered. My mother once told me that if you speak quietly, people have to work harder to hear you, and they'll pay better attention to your words.

Seven

BRAND ME

I am holding my friends' two small cherubic twins, a boy and a girl; I don't want to let the girl go.

"If it gets overwhelming, I'll take one," I tell them. I am serious.

They laugh. "No, but you can go get your own."

They hand me a slip of paper with a phone number written on it.

The babies vanish, and I wake from the dream.

By the summer of 2009, I'd had a series of baby dreams. In all of them, I woke up feeling an intense love for the children and then a profound loss upon consciousness that they weren't real. But the dream felt like a pulse from the universe, a sign from a soul to go. Keep going. That baby was out there.

The agency I chose, the Kinship Center, specialized in open adoptions, meaning that they encourage contact between the birth family and the adoptive family. This sounded right to me. I didn't ever want this child to have fantasies about her parentage—original or otherwise. I didn't ever want to be a block between a birth mom and her child. Open adoption is better, anyway, for the mental health of all involved. Kinship felt like my people.

I learned from the training and through the people who came to talk to us that there are about a hundred kinds of sadnesses intrinsic to adoption and foster care. For adoptive parents, a big one is the loss of fertility, where the dream of carrying and birthing a child is either slowly eroded, one negative pregnancy test after another or through a string of miscarriages, or dashed completely against rocks with a single proclamation from a medical professional that you are unable to create or carry a child. For birth parents, the sadness is most obviously the loss of the child and, maybe for some, a shattering reality check about their capabilities and choices. For the adoptee, it's relinquishing the mother you knew from the inside out as you formed into a person and then, later, whatever ideas you may have had about your original family. There are many, many shades of loss in between those major hues.

Often, people fear the concept of open adoption if they don't quite understand the dynamics of the human heart when it's wrenched away from family, no matter how vile or brutal or hopeless the surrounding circumstances. They think that somehow it will be easier for everyone if the adoption is tucked away onto a dark shelf on top of the closet, never to be acknowledged. But as we now know, the seed of identity, of knowing, of desire for the correct origin story will sprout even under the most airtight, closed-off conditions.

Closed adoptions are more of a modern phenomenon than you might expect. I talked with Kathleen Silber, an author and activist who pioneered the nation's movement toward open adoption in the late 1970s. "Open adoption was more than normal, but it was the family or church or community that would make arrangements, and people knew who everybody was, so there wasn't any secrecy," she said. "Then came a time period in the early part of the last century when there seemed to be a stigma to illegitimacy."

For a good part of the twentieth century, birth certificates were marked "illegitimate" or "bastard" if the baby's parents weren't married. In order to better escape that stigma, birth certificates were sealed, ostensibly to protect the birth mother's identity and to help the child with a home placement. "Besides the stigma of illegitimacy, there was a stigma to being barren, and if you were barren, there was something wrong with you. You're cursed by God," Silber said.

An indelible yearning for knowledge eclipses the positive, protective intentions of closed adoptions. Adoptees need to know their story and that they weren't "given away" because of something they were or did; birth parents need to fully grieve and know their children are OK; adoptive parents need to fill in the blanks about their child's prehistory and help answer their questions. Secrecy equals shame. Illumination is powerful medicine.

Over time, researchers realized what everyone in the adoption triangle already knew from their own experiences—that it's healthier for all involved, in most situations, when there's at least some information exchanged between the adoptive family and the birth family.

The catalyst for much of this consciousness raising was Alex Haley's bestselling 1976 novel, *Roots*, and the ensuing television miniseries about an African boy, Kunta Kinte, kidnapped into US slavery.

"The whole country at that point became fascinated with their roots," Silber said. Adoptees, especially, wanted to know more about their original families, and most of the time, the door was slammed in their faces.

As a direct result of the *Roots* obsession, groups such as the Adoptees' Liberty Movement Association (ALMA) started to advocate for adoptees' rights, Silber said. "I went to some of the meetings of this ALMA group to listen to adoptees speaking out, because up to that point, I just assumed that we placed the babies, everybody lived happily ever after, that was fine."

Another organization, Concerned United Birthparents (CUB), also emerged in the mid-'70s, when Lee Campbell, a birth mother, attended an adoption support group and realized that birth parents had different loss issues than the others in the adoption triad. Today CUB is a national organization that provides resources to birth parents.

The adoptees Silber heard from said that even though they had had good upbringings and, for the most part, loved their families, they had a deep, indelible desire to know more about themselves. "It was like a missing puzzle piece and it was important to their identity," Silber said. "It was at that point that I decided that . . . we needed to start making changes in practice to promote better mental health for children, that they had the right to know the information about themselves."

Silber would go on to redefine adoption across the country with her book *Dear Birthmother*, which advocated for open channels between the birth parents and the adoptive family. It was the first time anyone would start to think about the feelings and well-being of birth mothers in a meaningful, public way.

Silber said that as soon as she started advocating for thoughtful policies and unlocking information to help adoptees, it became clear very quickly that open adoptions were better for all involved, even the adoptive parents. "By the birth parents being involved and actually picking the parents and them getting to know each other, I think that really freed up adoptive parents to feel like this was their child, that they didn't steal this baby from somebody or it wasn't a flip of the coin somewhere; that this child was meant to be their child because his birth mother had picked them and [it] was a permission to be parents. They also lost the fear of this unknown birth mother that they would have imagined to be lurking in the shadows, ready to grab their kid and run," she said. "That was really powerful. We didn't anticipate that beforehand, but we saw that very quickly."

The benefit to the birth parents was peace of mind about where their baby was going and how he or she was thriving—"Not feeling that they just abandoned their baby to an agency and the social workers and not knowing what happened to their baby. Even though they would go through a grief experience in placing a baby for adoption. It was just natural, and in all situations that happens, but they worked through the feelings of grief much more quickly and easily because they picked the parents. They knew who they were. They felt confident in their choice for parents, so we again quickly discovered for birth parents, too, that this was healthier," Silber said.

It is amazing to me that one woman operating by the sheer force of compassion would go on to change not only how the adoption process is normalized today but the lives of tens (if not hundreds) of thousands of the forgotten, scorned, and selfless birth parents who placed their children and the children who just wanted—no, needed—to know about them.

There were nineteen of us in the class that first Kinship session—eight couples and three single women—crammed into the fluorescent-lit conference room with its squiggle-print carpet, walls lined by cheery pictures of children and their families. I recognized some of my cohorts from the orientation session a couple weeks before. We'd taken the first step toward our adoption commitment; most of us would go through the next months—or years—together, gathering our mental and logistical bearings, getting fingerprinted, taking infant CPR classes, tackling mountains of paperwork, learning how to be adoptive parents. There was a gay couple I privately nicknamed Boy Band because they were so young and chiseled. Another couple, two women cops, were hilarious, cracking jokes like the bad kids in class, and I loved them instantly. Some suburban types. Two Indian women and their husbands, who could no longer adopt from their home country. Each person came into the room every month with their own unique pain print, their particular loss, and their own brand of wanting.

One couple I thought of as RenFair (and I do like Renaissance fairs and empire waists, by the way) wore purple almost exclusively. He had a formidable salt-and-pepper Barry Gibb heft of hair and goatee; she, a long, straight Crystal Gayle mane. Each session, they played out a version of the same scene:

"We can offer a child so many opportunities," he said.

She sniffled, dabbing tears from behind her big, round glasses, and was mostly quiet.

"We have lived abroad. We designed our own home and are very well versed in architecture. We are musicians and give special healing classes to children. Our opportunities for this child, they're endless."

One class I started counting how many times he said the word *opportunity* and stopped after I hit ten. Isn't adopting a child about building a family, not just doing someone some gigantic favor? How was the social worker reading them? I wondered, mentally ranking all of us in terms of birth-parent desirability.

Our social worker told us the most successful adoptive parents are the ones who "aren't bound by negatives." I guessed that would include me and my judgment of the others, which was always shallow, mostly wrong, and occasionally veered into mean-spiritedness.

A panel of birth mothers came to our second class. They shared stories of abandonment and loss, being treated differently at the hospital, without compassion, without an acknowledgment that what they were doing was the most soul-wrenching act of love a human can put forth.

One birth mom said that after she read about one hundred profiles, it seemed like everyone lived on a cul-de-sac and had a guard dog and an SUV. She ended up choosing the couple who'd provided pictures of themselves with underwear on their heads, because she wanted the child she bore to grow up having fun.

"The three things that will kill your adoption plan are fear, pain, and secrets," said Melissa, the agency's director. Which can apply to everything, no matter what it is or who you are. Like the would-be mom who didn't tell the agency about her DUI, and when they ran the background check, they told her she had to wait another year before she was eligible to adopt.

Sometimes, though, newly minted parents would come in, victorious in their sleeplessness, carrying their newborn outfitted in the cutest, softest pajamas. They'd tell their story: "It was a complete surprise! We had only four hours to get ready!" or "We'd been talking to the birth mom for a while, and it looked like she was going to change her mind but then she didn't, and here we are." And infinite variations. And each time, the rest of us looked upon that child for the small miracle she was for that family and the hope she represented for us. We'd go in turn, telling our stories of impatience, dashed dreams, family members who couldn't comprehend our journey. We'd hold space for each other but always, invariably look longingly, wistfully at the child. "We're next, maybe," I'd tell myself, imagining the day when I could also introduce my new child to this unlikely tribe of hopefuls.

Once, at a support group, I announced that our adoption was finalized. There was an audible gasp from the crowd as I pulled out an eight-by-ten photo of the new baby—a Chihuahua my neighbor found on the Interstate 5. We'd taken him in and named him Cinco. There were relieved giggles but not the outburst of laughter I'd envisioned. Like making a disaster joke too soon after the bombing dust had settled.

I made friends with one couple in our group, Amala and Ben. They worked in tech and were cheerful and fun and friendly, and I was happy to know people who were having a similar experience at the same time. She was Indian and he was Japanese American, and only a few months into their adoption process, they met a young, pregnant

Filipina who had taken an immediate liking to them. A couple weeks later, their baby was born, looking just like a blend of them, which was so uncanny. Or maybe wasn't. I have a theory on why families through adoption sometimes look alike: The first reason is because we are so wired to look for patterns when we meet families; our brains piece together a physical origin story. And also because maybe birth parents on a conscious or unconscious level choose people who remind them of their biological family.

Several months in, a new couple joined our support group, and they got matched before they even finished their paperwork. She was Vietnamese and he Caucasian. The birth mother wanted a Vietnamese family.

I felt like the weird experimental cereal flavor, still on the shelf, that ends up at the 99 Cents Only Store (oh hi, pumpkin-spice Cheerios!). Nobody had asked about me. This was not for lack of trying.

The parent profile is like a sales sheet that explains in limited words and lots of pictures to a prospective birth parent why I'd be the perfect choice as a mother for her child. I'd created several versions of my profile, first alone and then again once Peter came into the picture after we'd broken up, reunited, and got engaged.

For my first attempt, I decided to design it like a skin-care product package, all green and white and flowery, because I am attracted to skin-care packages and why wouldn't all women be? The "hero" image of me has my hair with the bad bang trim blowing in the wind and a tentative smile on my face. Below that, photos of me riding Shi-Shi the camel ("I'm adventurous!") in Israel and a picture of me posing with a Bob the Builder–costumed mascot ("I'm a little wacky!"). On the flip side, a sweet picture of me with my mother ("I love my family!"), me walking the dog ("See, I can keep something alive!"), and a couple of pictures of me looking very engaged with my friends' daughters ("I can so totally relate to children!"). In the end, the flowery green accents overpowered the photos and the very sincere seven-paragraph essay on my background and why I'd be a great mom ("I will share the most important things that my parents gave me: generosity of spirit; unconditional love; intellectual curiosity; a passion for books, art, and music; respect and reverence for nature; a love of travel and the awareness it brings; and extreme compassion and appreciation for the grand parade of humanity and its goofballs, shining stars, and unsung heroes").

Once Peter came on board and we were officially married in the late summer of 2010, we needed to rebrand. Our initial joint effort resulted in a four-page fold-out brochure in blue and white, colors that lent credibility. The first page was an image of us freshly married, looking wistfully over a lake, my long auburn hair extensions cascading just so over my shoulder. We jammed it with pictures of camping ("We're nature-y!"), family and friends ("When you pick us, your kid gets all these bonus people!"), fun facts ("Vanessa has appeared on four game shows and won on two of them! Peter was a state motorcycle champion at the age of ten. He was also the only one competing in that category!"), and us in our natural habitats ("Peter plays guitar! Here's Vanessa, paws up in Japan with the prosperity cat!"). It's all an exercise in marketing your very core being in mostly pictures and very few words—not for the wishy-washy, verbose, or someone who tries to be everything for everyone.

I started putting the word out about my adoption. I sent a mass email to everyone I knew with the link to my profile and made posts on Facebook and tweeted it. My friends shared it, and I basked in the glow of support and encouragement. I heard back from one Chicago friend whose teenage daughter had a pregnant classmate and forwarded the link, but that was the end of it.

During my last two brief pregnancies I'd discovered BabyCenter.com, a clearinghouse of information for parents—mostly women—at all stages of baby having. On the site, you could track your baby's development from the size of a grain of rice to a Roma tomato to a large cabbage, as well as crowdsource information on every possible spot, itch, smell, and lump on you or your child. In addition to the exhaustive trove of knowledge, BabyCenter hosted thousands of forums for like-minded people at all stages of their parenthood journey. I found a group for pregnant teenagers and assumed that some of them would be debating placing their child for adoption. I monitored the posts for a few nights and saw my opportunity when one young woman posted that she wasn't sure if she wanted to keep her baby or not and was getting pressure from her family to decide.

I replied to her in a public post on the forum:

"Hi. I see this is a very confusing and difficult time for you. It's important to know that you have so many rights as a mother giving birth in the adoption process. You can wait until after the baby is born to decide—never let anyone pressure you to make a choice that is not fully yours.

"If you ever seriously consider adoption as an option, know that there are so many people who would be willing to love and raise that child. I'm a hopeful adoptive parent. Here's our profile if you're ever interested."

I thought it was a fair, supportive response.

But nobody else did, and they let me know it with a barrage of responses and direct emails. A couple of the more pointed communiqués included:

"How dare you approach vulnerable teenagers and suggest the only option available to them is adoption? In case you haven't noticed, the Pregnant Teenagers group on BabyCenter is for SUPPORT. Support in HAVING our children. Not in giving them up. You really should have done your research. I wish you all the luck in the world finding a child to adopt. I actually wish I had one FOR you to adopt, as I know the struggles one faces in trying to conceive. But preying on teenagers is an absolutely horrible thing to do."

And, "Do you realize you sound like a recent baby-hungry woman that sliced open the belly of another woman for her child? Instead of trolling the Internet looking for someone to child snatch, why don't you look for reputable adoption agencies and do it the legal way?"

I fielded dozens of comments for forty-eight hours straight. In the beginning they were on BabyCenter—and I started apologizing profusely and trying to explain myself, until the moderator banned me from the site. Turns out, by offering adoption as an option, I'd offered an incredibly predatory sentiment. There were a few other women, from time to time, who'd tried to approach the group in the same way. The girls and women in that group are hypersensitive to this kind of thing, as they should be.

The backlash singed my eyelashes and turned my skin a deep, dark red. My stomach warped in embarrassment, and my shoulders turned in for shame.

I also tried another tactic born out of being impatient, low, and verging on desperate after two years of waiting. Taken in by the promotional video of the young, happy couple and their beautiful baby boy, and against the advice of my agency social worker, I paid a woman who had an adoption-marketing agency $4,200—pretty much the bulk of my savings—to promote my profile (plus there was another $300 to her designated graphic designer, who made a crafty scrapbook-themed version). There were zero results from this and a "sorry, we don't offer refunds" when I asked for one.

The only real bite Peter and I got was one Saturday morning when I answered a call from the social worker: a college student had just given birth to a baby boy in Long Beach, an hour away. My heart stopped. I may have peed a tiny bit in my pants. "There's just one thing," Linda, the social worker, said. "The father is schizophrenic. You're going to have to weigh this very carefully. Can you get back to us in an hour?"

Peter and I rushed around the house in confusion. We called our mothers, who were supportive without giving us direction either way. We learned from quick Internet searches that there was a 13 percent chance the baby could also be schizophrenic. That boys suffer from schizophrenia more than girls. I called my girlfriend Joanna, who had just received her PhD in psychology. She said the child would never have a normal life. I imagined wondering, as he got older, if a temper tantrum was just a normal kid thing or if it was something deeper.

It felt like too big a decision to make in just an hour. As much as we wanted a baby, and as much faith as we had in the process, we just didn't know enough. Another couple from our agency got the same call as they were visiting Santa Barbara, a good three hours' drive away. As the wife talked on the phone to the social worker, a whale breached in the ocean in front of her and a rainbow appeared. She knew this child was her baby, and she drove like hell down the coast to meet him. It was supposed to be this way. She brought him in his soft-skinned, cherubic perfection to the next support group, and I felt truly happy for all of them.

In the spring of 2011, I was in cruise mode at my job, still doing good work as a PR flack for the company's renewable energy and energy-efficiency efforts, though John, my favorite boss, had left, and a management shift and political infighting had damaged department morale. I shepherded in the company's social-media efforts but was passed over to manage them in favor of a younger, more buttoned-up white man.

Corporate America stopped making sense to me, and all the rules seemed so arbitrary—you had to show up in the office, even if you didn't need to be there and could work just fine from home. You had to wear certain clothes and play hierarchy games. Lip service was given to creativity, but failure, a more common by-product of innovative thinking, was harshly reprimanded, even though it's widely known that Thomas Edison tried at least one thousand times before he got the light bulb right and up to ten thousand times before perfecting the alkaline battery.

Once, I'd worked hard on a presentation and was looking forward to showing it to some executives. It went flawlessly; they expressed admiration for the thoughtful innovation I displayed. Then one of them said, "Now you can get back to the kitchen."

I laughed along with them, dying inside, mortified. Some micro-bullshit too tiny to call out, too huge to forget.

One Friday afternoon I was in my dull grey cubicle, pondering dinner, wondering how early I could leave without being noticed. A call from Linda, the social worker, came in. After two years of filling out paperwork, chasing wispy, insignificant leads, wondering if every single call I ever got would be *the* call, there it was.

"There's a young woman, very pregnant, but nobody's sure when she's due," Linda said. "Her name is Bridgett. She's Caucasian, twenty-three years old, having a girl. She seems really nice but shy. Her boyfriend, Bill, is a piece of work, though."

A note on Bill: I would learn that there are wildly inconsistent chronologies in the stories he tells. His dates don't align for the years he assigns to his birth, schooling, military service, and other life events. I don't know what the absolute truth is and, really, if it matters at all in the grand scope of things. However the facts are skewed, I'm certain he believes it's for his protection and survival.

Linda went on to say that they'd burned through one arrangement already and had missed most of the prenatal appointments that had been set up for them—now Bridgett was having trouble finding an ob-gyn who would take her, penniless, without insurance. "She is high risk," Linda said.

Still. I wanted to meet this Bridgett. I called her, and she answered in a quiet voice, like someone who hadn't spoken all day, or longer. Peter and I arranged to pick her up that evening outside the downtown Los Angeles apartment she now shared with Bill. Bill was at work.

We parked the car, texted Bridgett that we were there, and waited downstairs for what seemed like an interminably long time. It crossed my mind, as people came and went from the lobby—mostly young hipsters, artist types—that I'd not an inkling what she looked like. And then there she was. Of course I recognized her: a white girl, long hair down to her waist, parted in the middle. Not blonde, not brown, a color my mother would probably call ash, though I don't know if people use that term anymore. Big hazel-green eyes behind gold-rimmed John Lennon glasses. Reed-thin limbs, faded jeans, a white peacoat, too short in the arms, that stretched out over a basketball of a belly.

What do you say to the woman who might be the mother of your child? Do you hug? Handshake? I did one that melted into the other.

"Well," I said, in the amped-up cheery tone I do when I'm nervous, sounding like a recording of myself, "where shall we eat? What's good around here?" None of us could think of anything off the top of our heads that would be walkable for a woman with a baby coming any time, so we ducked inside the burger joint in front of us.

You'd think that it would all come naturally when you're meeting your destiny. That the universe greases your wheels when you're on the right track. That most everything is already written. That we have so little control over what others think and do and feel, that the Fates will play as they may. Still, this encounter posed a make-or-break moment, the most important interview of my life. I tried hard to remember everything we'd learned in the classes about meeting a birth mom: Make sure that you show you care about her, not just the baby. Ask about her life. Relax, be yourself. Everything we talked about felt like small talk. I couldn't tell how we were registering with her. She was so quiet.

Bridgett hesitated when she answered questions with her sweet, barely audible voice, almost like a time delay in a call with spotty reception. I was wildly curious about her. My thought train careened as I tried to remain calm: Am I supposed to keep talking? Will she say something? Wait, there she goes, she's talking! I sent telepathic messages to Peter, who was letting me lead: Where are you? Can you participate more?—Does she like us? I think she likes us—then, aaak, Peter, why did you have to tell that story about the band breaking up when you were twenty? Nobody cares.

We talked about where she was from, what she liked to do, how she met Bill. After all her grocery experience in Ohio, she'd still not been able to land a job in LA. About their pet rabbit they called Ynnub (*bunny* spelled backwards), which they'd gotten a couple months prior. I wondered if it was for a preemptive softening of the blow, knowing they'd give up their own baby. But it felt like too personal a question to ask. Bridgett tore into her food ravenously, unapologetically, as a pregnant woman should. I liked that. I wanted to feed her more. I wanted to protect her. I wanted to know her.

A blob of bright-yellow mustard spilled onto her white coat. "Spic and Span will take that out," she said. I would later learn that Bridgett is a fount of practical information like this: how to substitute Splenda for sugar in baking, how to get the best coupons, how to create elaborate meals using a microwave and a hot plate.

Peter and Bridgett found common conversational ground in music. Peter, a one-time regional rock star, had been the front man for the Southern California equivalent of Duran Duran in the early 1980s. They'd played at the '84 Olympics.

We talked a little about the baby. Bill made her a green protein shake every morning. She thought the baby would come soon. She said they couldn't be parents because they wanted to focus on their music. It wasn't the right time for them.

When we finished eating and wandered out to the sidewalk, the elephant ghost question hung over our heads. Did she like us? Did she want us to become parents to the basketball?

"I want you to talk to Bill," she said, taking out her prepaid Blackberry phone. After a few words with him, she handed the phone to me.

Bill seemed more outgoing, blessed with the gift of gab. We talked briefly about his work, then he said, "If Bridgett is happy with you guys, then I'm happy."

It seemed easy. Too easy. I kept grasping for what to do next and realized there was no playbook, no app you could look up to figure out what the protocol was. We were winging it in live time. We decided to have dinner together that Sunday.

Peter and I went home, buoyed by hope. This might actually work.

That night, I felt cautious. Bill and Bridgett's decision seemed so quick. Was this too good and easy to be true? They had given us no reason to believe they would change their minds. But I'd heard so many stories about people coming this close to the agreement, and then the birth parents reversed and made their own little family happen, despite the obstacles.

I was quiet and hopeful. Then, around ten p.m., an email from Bill popped into my inbox. It said the adoption with the previous woman had fallen through because she was stingy and unhelpful to them when they needed her most. And that they were flat broke. "We sleep on dirty sheets because we don't even have the money to do laundry right now. And Bridgett lactates EVERY night if you get my drift. But this has to all go down next week, and I am going to be frank in letting you know we are not going to ask you for money. If you help us out, then you have our word we will NOT let the adoption fall through." He said he was worried that their relationship would be destroyed if they had to raise a child together and that they wanted to get back on track with their lives as soon as possible. "If you want this little girl that Bridgett is carrying, then it is yours if you are willing to get involved right NOW!"

I read the email over and over again. I balked. My first instinct was to slow down, as I am always wary of hard sells and high-pressure tactics.

I wasn't choking so much because they asked for help—after all, I'd expected to provide support for a birth parent—but because of the hard-sell nature of it, the acceleration of the decision process. Bill felt like a force of nature. Wow, we would have to deal with this guy the rest of our lives if we go through with this, I thought.

But this was not a car dealership, where the same model could be found at a different place down the road the next week. This was a couple having a baby. Any day now. Bill was right. There was no time to "date" each other before we took the plunge.

I forwarded the note to Linda, the social worker, and my friend Joanna, the psychologist, for their input. They both got back to me immediately. "He sounds like a man backed into a corner," said Joanna. Which was exactly what he was. Linda gave me another kind of reality check when she said that you get the baby and the bathwater, together. Bill would always be in the picture, actively or completely hidden, but there somewhere nonetheless. I showed Peter the note, but he turned all the decisions over to me.

My indecision felt like a vise, a corset, a straightjacket. My mind went blank. But there was something operating in my subconscious that said, "Don't. Don't say anything yet." I decided to wait a day to respond, which, although I advise others to employ the same restraint in a situation requiring delicacy, is very unlike me.

I trudged off to bed as thoughts about Bill and Bridgett and the reality of the situation scrambled about in my mind. As my head hit the pillow, I got a message from somewhere deep in my brain, a subconscious section that wants me to win, to succeed, to save myself, to do the very rightest thing. I don't always tune into this signal, but that night, I did. I'd been reading the Dalai Lama, who talks about how it is easy to be compassionate to someone you like, to your friends. But the work of compassion is to extend it to your enemies or to those who are difficult. The full thought is: "Every single being, even those who are hostile to us, is just as afraid of suffering as we are, and seeks happiness in the same way we do. Every person has the same right as we do to be happy and not to suffer. So let's take care of others wholeheartedly, of both our friends and our enemies. This is the basis for true compassion."

It would be trite to call it an aha moment. It was a very small thought in my sleepy mind to turn judgment about Bill's note into compassion.

I mentally, emotionally, and spiritually reframed everything in the context of how to serve this couple, this child. The next day, I wrote to Bill and Bridgett and offered to help them with their rent, regardless of whether they chose us as the baby's parents or not. I told them we'd also help with next month's rent, plus any groceries, phone cards, and other expenses during the month if they did want to keep talking about choosing us as parents. They were fine with this and accepted without hesitation—it was actually a little arresting that there was no back-and-forth. I've negotiated more at the farmers market buying soy candles. But this was no ordinary deal. Not a thing, a person. We each needed something desperately.

On Sunday, I fretted over what to wear, with the little knowledge I had about them. Something earthy enough and relatable for hippie musicians but pulled together enough to show responsibility. I settled on a short yellow linen dress with cowboy boots.

We picked them up and drove to a Mexican restaurant in East LA—a place Peter chose for its authenticity, in hopes that it would resonate well with Bill, to appeal to his Texan and Mexican roots.

Over burritos bigger than our heads, we talked about where they'd been and things they'd done. Bill thought that maybe he'd seen Peter perform live in North Hollywood. We knew he hadn't, because it had been years since Peter had stepped foot there, but didn't say anything. It wasn't until we stuffed ourselves and the plates were cleared that Peter finally asked for some confirmation, and I was grateful for his question, the one I couldn't bring myself to ask. "So . . . are you cool with us being the parents?"

Bill and Bridgett nodded enthusiastically. Yes. It was on. We took them home. "I think we have a baby," Peter said. We'd be our own family.

I was stunned, spooked, and hopeful. I was in love with Peter and our future.

For the next several days, I traveled in a careful bubble, no sudden moves and no loud noises. I knew my new reality could burst at any time. I just wanted to keep it afloat, full of promise and wonder. I told only a close friend or two, not wanting to jinx it, not wanting to answer questions or hand back the gift of a soft baby blanket if it didn't work out.

Eight

LIFE BLOOMS IN ROCKY SOIL BECAUSE OF IT AND IN SPITE OF IT

I am a naturally curious person, but when it came to Bill and Bridgett, I was ravenous for information about them. Mostly because I just wanted to know, to have some clues about what had led them to this moment of living in the cheapest SRO in the city, reaching for stars they knew were out there somewhere, and having a baby due any time with an uncertain future. But I also wanted to know in case they ever disappeared, so I would have something to tell this child about who they were.

Bill says he doesn't have a birth certificate, and he's not even sure exactly where he was born. His father, William; William's wife, Martha (Bill refuses to acknowledge her as his mother), whom Bill described as cruel—let him know very little about his early life. The one thing his father did do for him was to talk him into visiting the armed forces recruiter. At seventeen, Bill joined the navy.

You'd think a hippie, guitar-slinging, late-sleeping kid would hate being in the military. But it was the exact opposite—at first. "If they'd left us in Virginia Beach, I'd still be in the navy to this day, I'd refuse to leave. But I went to the submarines instead and worked on nuclear missiles. We were down for three months underwater and up for three. The exact opposite of Virginia Beach is a submarine. Worse than the exact opposite, it's like hell," Bill said. "I spent three years in the navy. And I'm glad I did, it was good for me to do that. It was a great learning experience, but I still missed Texas, my friends, the music, the land."

Bill's life has been marked by extremes: cruelty and kindness, poverty and wealth, talent and ineptitude, luck and tragedy. He was close to his grandmother, the woman who'd taught him piano at the age of three, the person who'd shown him the most kindness and who'd given him the gift of music.

Perhaps his most important pivot came in the late '80s, when he got a call from old friends in a Tejano crossover band called the Texas Tornadoes. They hung out, jammed on guitar and vocals, and wrote a song called "Hey Baby Que Paso" that would become a 1990 hit.

Hoping to build on his success, Bill followed the band to Los Angeles, bunking down in the cheapest place possible, a residential hotel downtown called the Cecil, where a room cost $450 a month with a student ID. And then, as it happens, the situation imploded and the band went back to Texas. Bill wanted to stay in LA—now that his grandmother was gone, there was nothing for him back in the Hill Country except for a scrubby landscape and a few friends. The stars faded quickly from Bill's eyes, and he ended up working as an assistant manager at a Pizza Hut, as he had in Texas. He also joined Myspace, where he promoted the music from a band he'd been in, Paramount Blues Review. There, in the miasma of electricity and information and interconnected servers and music and hopes and art and self-promotion and adoration, he connected with a young woman named Bridgett.

As a child growing up in Milford, Ohio, Bridgett was shy and timid, sensitive and bright. Whether she let on or not, she knew every nuance happening in any room. She shared a simple brick home with her mother and grandmother, Molly—her father was on the road as a truck driver most of the time, and she didn't have a lot of interaction with him early on. She bonded more closely with her grandmother. Her mother, Bridgett thought, was too much of a teenager herself to raise a child.

Molly, jolly in a Mrs. Claus way, with a smile that took over her whole face, was a career worker at Burger King. But when she was around, she'd love Bridgett in the way nobody else would. She'd never get mad. They'd watch *The Lion King* on repeat. They'd make art and play games and do music together. Mostly, Bridgett remembers Molly's soft body, always good for a hug. But one day that heart that gave out so much pure love just plain gave out. And Bridgett felt even more alone with her mother than if she had actually been by herself. Bridgett immersed herself in school and got good grades. She drew anime-style cartoons compulsively. But whatever force field Molly had provided had evaporated. Bridgett no longer wanted to be home. She didn't trust her mother. She didn't feel safe around the crazy mood swings.

At sixteen, Bridgett moved in with her dad and stepmother in Princeton, Indiana, which she described as a small, boring town. Whatever hopes she had for a better, new life faded soon after she got there. Maybe there wasn't enough room, not just in the house but also in their life. She and her dad became at odds.

So Bridgett moved out, earned her GED, and then, finally, felt like her life had started. Her job at Wendy's provided interaction with the world and a paycheck. In her off time, she started teaching herself the bass guitar and losing herself listening to music. But she was lonely. She'd never been able to shake the shyness from her childhood. It felt hard to meet people—even though Bridgett, as a friend, was one of the most loyal and solid people you could ever have in your life.

She found her way back to Ohio and took a job in a Kroger supermarket, and then discovered bodybuilding. She liked how the weights made her strong, how her body changed as time passed. How she went from skinny all over to muscled and cut. She liked how people might think twice about messing with her when they saw how strong she was.

Bridgett started living in a parallel universe on Myspace as Ms. Muscle, exploring bands, watching videos for hours at a time. She made friends. The most important one would be Bill.

By 2009, Bill and Bridgett were writing back and forth several times a day, talking about things important and mundane. They sent each other pictures of what they were doing, and moved off Myspace and began texting each other. Sometimes they'd be at it for twenty-four-hour stretches.

For Bridgett, who'd never had what she considered a real boyfriend, this felt romantic and exciting. For Bill, it was at first a case of mistaken identity—he thought Ms. Muscle was the sister of one of his band-mates. And then he realized Bridgett was Bridgett.

Two years into their online courtship, Bill asked if Bridgett would like to make a band with him. She said yes—she'd been entertaining the idea of coming to Los Angeles as well. Bill turned her on to Westwood College—it's closed now, after it bilked a bunch of people out of money—as a place to go for paralegal classes. He had enrolled at a place called Abraham Lincoln University, an online law school with a Los Angeles campus. Both of them were interested in becoming lawyers or, at least, fending off anyone who wanted to bring trouble.

Bridgett didn't want to stare down a future of herself as a supermarket clerk in Ohio. She wanted a city. Something else, something bigger. She told her mother and her cousin, who was also her best friend, that she was moving to LA. Don't, they said. You'll be sold into white slavery.

But Bridgett didn't see how staying in that nothing Ohio town with nothing going on would be much better.

When she'd saved $5,000 from the grocery job, she texted Bill, "I'm coming to LA." She got on a Greyhound bus. She was so nervous she didn't sleep very well during the three days it took to get there. That was the summer of 2010. She was twenty-two.

Los Angeles was its hot, grimy summer self that day. Bridgett disembarked the bus to see Bill there, waiting for her. She thought he looked just like his picture. She knew him immediately. She also knew at that moment that she would spend her life with him. There was even a feeling of being together before, somehow.

"Hi, Bill," she said.

At that moment, everything changed for them. For all of us.

Bill brought her home to his tiny studio, where she put her stuff down and washed up. They ate sushi, and he gave her a walking tour of downtown and all the places where she could get a cheap apartment. She filled out a couple rental applications.

Initially, he was more interested in a bandmate than a real-life relationship with her—he'd been through a parade of bassists and drummers over the past several months. He thought she was pretty but too bulky from working out. But also, he didn't have a lot of other romantic business going on at that time.

That first night, Bridgett slept over. Bill's room was barely big enough for a bed, but he cleared a spot for her on the floor. Bridgett got in the bed anyway, and they consummated their online relationship in real life, despite whatever doubts Bill had.

Bridgett stayed the next night. And the night after. A few nights later, as they made love in their little nest, they felt something different. It was as if a little spirit came in and just went "whoop!"

That little "whoop" was forgotten—until she made herself known. Bridgett and Bill went along building their life together, making a band and going through more drummers than Spinal Tap, Bridgett looking unsuccessfully for work, Bill racking up hours. One day in February, Bridgett looked down at her belly. It'd gone from flat like a board to a big bump overnight. She didn't have normal periods anyway, so she hadn't been suspicious anything was amiss. There was no morning sickness nor any other pregnancy symptoms.

She stared in the mirror and cried.

There wasn't much discussion about keeping the baby. Bridgett and Bill were so close to the edge they were basically hanging off it;

an eviction was pending. They weren't ready to be parents. They had dreams to conquer.

Nights were tough. Bridgett couldn't sleep or get comfortable, her belly becoming huge on her frame, thin now that she wasn't bulking up in a gym anymore.

They knew another couple, heroin junkies, who had used the Kinship Center to place their baby for adoption. The adoptive parents had supported them through the pregnancy by giving them $1,000 a month, shuttling them back and forth to doctor's appointments, and paying their rent. Sounded good. Bill and Bridgett signed on.

The social worker, Linda, gave them her usual spiel about adoption, their rights, and what they could expect, then presented a folder full of hopefuls.

"Just pick one," Bill said. Linda looked to Bridgett, who nodded in agreement.

Linda chose a single woman, an FBI agent. The first meeting went well, everyone thought, but then things began to deteriorate. The woman haggled with them over support and wasn't available to take Bridgett to doctor's appointments, meaning Bill would need to take off a day of work to accompany her. Once, they were told that the only place that would accept their Medi-Cal card was in Long Beach. They took the train down, got to the clinic, and were told it was a mistake. Nobody could see them. They made it to only one prenatal appointment, where they were told Bridgett was having a girl and given some vitamins.

Bill and Bridgett asked Linda for another match, but Linda wanted them to see it through.

"I'm taking the rent money and sending Bridgett back to Ohio, then," Bill said.

Linda relented.

Nine

THERE IS NO PRECISE MOMENT WHEN YOU BECOME A PARENT

Three days after we'd met Bill and Bridgett, I had to travel for work to a conference in Monterey. I explained to my boss that the baby might come any day, and he said, "It would be a shame if you missed the trip and she ended up not having the baby. Besides, if it's her first, it will take a while. You'll have plenty of time to come back." He was a dad a couple times over, so maybe he believed this. Even though it was less than an hour's plane ride to the nearest airport, in San Jose, there would still be an hour's drive after that. And the reverse on the way back. Against my instincts, I went to Monterey.

Tuesday morning, I blew off the first conference session trying to wrangle a doctor's appointment for Bridgett, calling numbers the social worker had suggested I try. Bridgett was so far along hardly anyone would see her, especially since there was such a small pool of doctors serving women marginalized this way. It would take a specialist in her network.

Finally, I got confirmation that a doctor would see her next Thursday.

In my two years of waiting, I'd not purchased one diaper, one bottle, one onesie. I called my cousin Maggie, a new mom herself. "I think it's going to happen. I think we have a match. What do I do now?"

"Holy fuck," she said, and then rattled off everything I'd need, item by item, as I wrote furiously with a stubby pencil on the hotel room pad.

I had become so late for the conference that it really didn't matter anymore, but I got dressed and started to make my way out the door. And then I got a text from Bill.

"Bridgett's in labor. Send Peter."

At first this seemed to make sense. They had no car, so of course they'd want Peter to come. But then I realized, WHY ARE YOU CALLING PETER?! And then, JESUS CHRIST, YOU ARE HAVING A BABY, CALL 911!!!

Bill had panicked as he watched Bridgett's eyes roll back into her head with pain as she slumped down in the shower and briefly passed out. Unsure of what exactly was going on—or maybe because he thought it would get them there faster—he reached for the most critical-case scenario and ran with it. He called 911 and told the dispatcher she was in cardiac arrest.

They called their friend, neighbor, and temporary drummer, Teeny. She was a bespectacled, sylphlike slip of a woman, who worked as a stripper and had placed her own child for adoption years before with family members. Teeny was the only one in the room who had her head on straight and had figured out the baby's arrival was imminent. She went to the hospital with them.

I called Peter, who was at work at least a half hour away from Bridgett and Bill. He called 911. "There's a twenty-three-year-old woman in labor right now," he said, and gave the address.

The dispatcher responded, "We actually have a call in from that same address about a twenty-three-year-old woman in cardiac arrest."

Peter tried to explain. "Actually, they are probably the same person. She's having a baby. Really."

The medics arrived and shuttled Bridgett to the hospital.

Meanwhile, I got on the phone with the airline and summoned the spirit of my father, who never met a customer-service agent he couldn't bend to his will. "My baby is being born right now! I need to get on a plane from San Jose to Burbank!" I hyperventilated at the agent.

"Ma'am?"

I backed up and explained that yes, it was my baby but not coming *out* of me, that I was adopting, and I was offered the next flight out—but it was a good hour-plus ride to the airport. I got there with only moments to spare before departure. On the plane, anxious and willing time to warp, I wrote out a letter to this baby, whom I'd already decided (at about age twelve) to name Grace, after my father's mother.

> To our daughter,
>
> I am writing this on a plane, on my way to see you born. I hope I get there in time to watch you unfold and blossom into the world, a healthy, peaceful little girl. Our daughter. It is such a thrill to write that. Our daughter. I suspect it is a thrill that will never go away.
>
> You are a very special girl. So many people have loved you—your birth mother, Bridgett, and your birth father, Bill. Your dad and I have wanted you for such a long time. In fact, just last week we told you, "Come find us, we'll take it from there." We love you so much already and can't wait to meet you.
>
> I can't wait to find out what's happening. Peter, your dad, was on his way to be with you when I got on the plane.

I am sending a special message to God now, and hopefully writing it down will be a way for it to come through deeper and stronger:

May you arrive healthy and happy.

May you know love and peace from the moment you take your first breath, and forever after that.

May your angels keep close watch over you and protect you in a world filled with uncertainty.

May we be the best parents for you. We hope you'll never want for anything, that your life will be sunny and filled with beauty and wonder. That you will grow into a compassionate, funny, intelligent woman. We are proud of you already.

We are getting ready to land now, so I'm putting this notebook away. Little one, I can't wait to meet you. We will rock this world together.

Love,

Your mom

Meanwhile, Peter, who had already experienced baby waiting three times over, decided he'd have enough time to go home, walk the dog, and change his shirt. It was Bridgett's first, after all, and everyone says first babies take longer.

The plane landed, and I was digitally connected with the world again. A message popped up on my phone from Bridgett's number, sent by Teeny from the delivery room. It was one picture. A tiny, perfect, beautiful baby, screaming her life breath.

Peter had also missed the birth and arrived shortly after Bill, Bridgett, and Teeny had convened in the hospital room for baby meeting and recovery.

I hurried to the pickup curb, where my friend and next-door neighbor Sanjiv was supposed to be waiting for me but was nowhere to be seen. The texts from him started coming in.

"Leaving now."

"Ten minutes."

"Almost there."

If there was ever a time not to be late, this was it. When Sanjiv arrived, I was grateful for the ride but had nearly wriggled out of my skin. He'd delayed my baby-meeting time, an exquisite torture.

In the hospital, I navigated my way to the maternity ward. Bridgett was propped up in bed, pale and tired. Bill sat next to her, also looking worn, circles pronounced under his big brown eyes. Peter stood, holding a fussy little bundle of a person wrapped in a hospital-issued cotton blanket, white with a blue stripe. Her cries sounded more kitten than human. "Meet your baby," he said, handing her to me.

I don't know what I thought it would be like, seeing my child for the first time. Maybe something from a Hallmark commercial: tears of joy springing from my eyes as angel harp music, and perhaps a smattering of birdsong, wafted in from nowhere in particular. But it was none of that.

I held her in my arms, looking deep into her squishy, sweet face. I gently rocked her, and it felt like a dance. I realized only at that moment I'd had little to no experience with a newborn. It just felt right. Normal, no reason for tears. Only a very calm, solid kind of joy. My new normal. Me and this kid.

She stopped crying. "Hi, little one. Hi."

I looked at Bridgett. I'd worried about how much to claim motherhood around her. I didn't want to barge in on the precious time she had left in this role.

"Hold her as long as you want," Bridgett said.

"Come whenever you like, spend as much time as possible with her," Bill said.

They were like a border guard lifting a barrier, waving me through. Go. Be a mom.

For the next two days, I was fully in New Mommy Prep mode, tying up ends at work for my sudden maternity leave, sweeping Target for any possible baby needs as I checked items off the list my cousin Maggie had dictated. I popped into the hospital to visit Grace every chance I got.

Meanwhile, Bridgett was having her own new mom feelings about a baby who spent much of her time lying in a clear plastic box right next to her. She gave her the first name of Kelli, after a nice nurse who helped her, and Mae as a middle name, just because she liked the way it sounded. She knew the name would change. But for two days, Kelli Mae would be her given name. Given by her legal, biological mother. Nobody would take that away, at least, not yet. Up until then, she and Bill had referred to the baby as "the Bunny."

Peter and I went to see them as often as possible in those two extra days. At first the staff probably assumed we were family, but then they learned we were adopting Grace. They switched gears entirely. While they didn't show outward antagonism to us, they worked behind the scenes to pressure Bridgett into keeping the baby. Once, they separated Bridgett from Bill and took her into a little room on her own, telling her about the social services available to her, grilling her for two hours to make sure Bill wasn't spearheading the adoption decision. They tried to position the Kinship agency as the bad guy, facilitator of some ritualized baby snatching. "Look," the nurse said, "nobody from the agency even came to see you for a postpartum visit."

That was true. But Bridgett and Bill had given up on Kinship weeks before. They'd expected nothing and were still mad and disappointed when that was exactly what they got.

Still, hospital nurses pressed Bridgett to keep the baby and offered to call in social services and an attorney, even though all our paperwork was in order and signed. They threatened to put the child in foster care. It was as if they thought she'd have a different answer the hundredth time they asked. As if Bridgett were a child who didn't know her own mind. She didn't budge.

They stayed in the hospital that Tuesday, the night of the birth, and Wednesday night. On Thursday, it was time to go home. The hospital loaded up Bridgett and Bill with a free stroller and a baby starter kit with formula samples plus a few diapers.

We all piled into Peter's truck. Bridgett, Grace, and I were in the back seat, Bill in the front. Neither Bridgett nor I could stop looking at Grace, so sweet in her little blue-and-white hospital blanket, trying hard to stay awake. She kept falling asleep. It's a lot of work to be born, for both people involved.

We took a slow, quiet ride home. Peter and Bill took the bags out. Bill grabbed the stroller the hospital gave them and later sold it on Craigslist for forty dollars. Bridgett slept for three or four days straight.

Then Bill and Bridgett were able to restart their life together, with no baby at the epicenter of the relationship. They tried to get past it as quickly as they could. They went to the beach a couple weeks later and posted a picture on Facebook of Bridgett in a blue-green tankini, with skinny limbs and flat tummy, looking exactly the same as she did before she was showing, like nothing had happened. As if to show any family members or friends who may have been suspicious from Facebook photos that indeed, there was no baby, nothing out of the ordinary.

Later that summer, they went to the Beverly Hills Courthouse and got married, wearing matching Monster Energy drink T-shirts and jeans.

PART III

MOMMIES ARE PEOPLE, PEOPLE WITH CHILDREN

Ten

You Wing It in Live Time, Every Day

We said goodbye to Bill and Bridgett as they got out of the car. The last time Bridgett had left her apartment, she'd had a baby inside her. She was coming home without her baby. Our baby. Ours and theirs.

The first night home, all I could do was marvel at the tiny creature who was suddenly my family, whose blood and breath and skin would become as close as you can be to another human's without actually morphing together. I wrapped her in a new, soft cotton onesie, slipped pink baby mittens on her tiny fingers, and placed a polka-dot cotton hat on her head. One of my favorite pictures from that night is of her sleeping, absorbing her new life, on Peter's bare chest. They are bathed in a golden light from the bedside lamp. He is looking down at her, and they are together in an oasis of peace.

A few days later, she met our close friends and family. Peter's daughters came over and sat on the couch, beaming at their new sister as they held her dearly. We finally had something—or someone, actually—whom we could all rally around, whom we could love in common. The iciness had thawed, at least a little.

I remember the first months of being a mother more like an impressionist painting than a series of crisp snapshots. When I'd previously envisioned myself as a mother, somehow the shit tons of laundry didn't ever make it into the picture. Some days the height of my productivity, in addition to keeping the baby alive, was unloading the dishwasher. I certainly didn't get a book proposal done. (In my prebaby delusion, I'd chirpily announced to my therapist that during maternity leave I'd have time to write it *while the baby was napping.* Which was about forty minutes a stretch. Ha ha ha ha ha ha ha ha ha. Fool.) I'd take Grace on long, long walks in the California heat to the park a little more than a mile away, or to the shopping district, or just to nowhere in particular. Grace would fall fast asleep in her sling, wrapped around my middle, and every few minutes I'd poke her just to make sure she was still breathing.

On those walks, we'd sometimes take refuge from the daunting heat in the cool air of the clearance room at Anthropologie, and I'd carefully consider buying soft, basic T-shirts on sale, marked down to thirty-nine dollars from fifty-eight, which seemed, to my sleep-deprived mind, like a screaming deal. (I bought three.)

Peter would come home and ask what we'd done. Most days, honestly, I couldn't remember anything to tell him. But I would point to the empty dishwasher.

The day loomed when I had to go back to work, and suddenly I was one of those women who were supposed to "have it all"—a home and husband and career and child. I don't know if that's even possible. I think you can "have it some" or "have it most." But all? Not unless you work for a company that's radically family friendly, or not unless you work for yourself or have some kind of crazy good passive income situation.

We had been able to cobble together only about nine weeks' worth of leave with our vacation days and allowed benefits. Peter was hesitant to use his full paternity leave for fear of passive-aggressive retaliation from the company. There was no other option. I'd been working steadily since I was fourteen, and now I just didn't want to.

I felt a foreboding grief as the minutes ticked closer to the time I'd be sitting back in my little grey cubicle. Grace and I had been sticking to each other like clinging monkeys—I'd read somewhere that the first three months of a baby's life should be treated as the "fourth trimester" and took this very seriously, keeping her close during most of my waking and sleeping hours. I developed a low-level envy of women who could stay home while their husbands earned the bread.

I was completely demoralized reading about other first-world countries' generous maternity-leave policies while I furiously researched daycare options: This one was too industrial. That one didn't accept babies. Finally, we settled on a place in between home and work, across the street from Maddie's new place, where she sent her daughter. It was a literal mom-and-pop operation run by an elderly couple out of their modest home. When we went to meet them for the first time, they lovingly picked up Grace and cooed to her, and she seemed just fine with it. It was the best we were going to get.

I showed up back at work on the appointed day, and the reality wasn't as bad as I'd anticipated—dealing with coworkers and daily fires at the office seemed easy compared with trying to fill a day at home. I'd drag my sleep-deprived butt out of bed early, get ready for work, and then usually need to change outfits after a spit-up malfunction (usually Grace's). I'd chug through the day like a steam engine, skipping lunch and small talk, so I could get out and hold my baby as soon as possible.

Mom-ing came with a professional cost. Once, I was invited by the EPA's Energy Star division to make a presentation at their annual conference in North Carolina, something I would have normally, in pre-Grace life, accepted immediately. I looked closely at the invitation and saw that they wanted me to present three times, on three consecutive days. My heart sank. I couldn't imagine going that long without inhaling the sweet baby smell, bouncing Grace on my knee as I ate dinner, snuggling in bed with her, and slipping off into a dream together after the four a.m. feeding.

My heart broke into two uneven pieces, but the bigger one was full of Grace. I didn't go to the conference.

She was about six months old when a winter windstorm left half a million people in Southern California without power for an average of four or five days. Crews wrestled to clear massive trees that had downed and snarled power lines along nearly inaccessible paths. At work, our small team of media-relations staff was on overtime giving interviews and updates to the press. I was among the lucky ones to still have electricity, so I'd wake up for my daily report with a local radio station at five a.m., the phone on speaker, Grace gurgling during her morning feeding in my arms as I read the updates on air to the reporter. By day two, the reporter had worked Grace into the conversation, asking how she was doing that morning, and she'd become her own little character in the ongoing story. By day four, after another long night and early morning, I planned on coming into the office, but our day-care lady had no power due to the storm and felt like she was unable to safely watch the children. My eyes sore and my body ragged, I bundled up Grace and took her with me to the office so I could pick up my computer and bring it home and at least attempt to work.

I stepped off the elevator and made my way to my grey-and-purple cubicle. Grace seemed to understand office etiquette, never making a peep except for perhaps a delighted giggle as colleagues came by to say hi and entertain her as I gathered my things. The phone lines were lit brightly with stacked media calls, and the team and our receptionist were having trouble keeping up. Grace quietly lay on a blanket on the floor. I answered the phone to pitch in and help. A friend in a less busy department offered to watch her for a few minutes as I caught up.

And then someone, likely a person under intense pressure and riddled with their own exhaustion, reported the baby as a distraction, and our manager called me in and asked me to leave. My face reddened as

I tried to explain that I was just helping on a call, getting my computer so I could work. I fought tears, scooped up Grace, and headed down to my car.

Grace had always been a strong traveler since her first ride in her daddy's truck, but on this day, she wailed. I did everything I could do to calm her from the front seat, made sure she had a blanket, sang, offered toys and a bottle. Nothing worked.

Finally I took an exit, pulled over in a run-down, unfamiliar part of town, got in the back seat, and held her. We cried together.

That night, I had tickets to the Joffrey *Nutcracker*, in which my ten-year-old neighbor and BFF, Keya, was dancing as a snow angel. Peter was stuck working, so Grace and I put on our Christmas best and headed to the ballet.

We sat in the nosebleed section, getting the stink eye from the usher, who made sure I knew that if Grace made so much as a burp, we'd need to exit. Gracie settled in. The overture began, the lights dimmed, and guests began to arrive at Clara's party. The Snow Queen floated, amid sparkly drifts, to her king.

Ballet is perfect for a six-month-old, by the way, as it's all action and music, never a still moment, always changing light and something different to see. Grace was silently entranced on my lap for about twenty minutes, then settled into a deep sleep.

I thought about how my dad used to take me to the ballet and to musical theater performances—it was our thing—and I so wanted to share with him these perfect moments of peace and art and beauty strung together, the twinkling lights of the soul. I don't know exactly where my dad is in his postearthly days, but I like to think he is with us for times like that. For those two hours, Nutcrackerland, with its whirling dervishes and sexy peacock and queenly Sugar Plum Fairy, was eons away from my regular life of answering phones and getting things done. I could have sat there for days.

Eleven

DNA Finds Its Way Back to Itself

Grace, who had been walking only a few months and who had never met a set of steps she didn't like, was testing her gravitational center, doing quite well, on some cobalt-blue metal playground stairs that would carry her up to a slide. We were at a park in downtown Los Angeles, a few blocks from where Bill and Bridgett lived. I'd stayed connected with them via email and on Facebook—when I posted pictures of Grace, they almost invariably would give them a thumbs-up. I'd like their posts about their band and their music. I'd write them notes about Grace and send them holiday messages. I'd sent Bridgett a short kilt and manga-art T-shirt for performing. But after a year and a half, this was the first actual in-real-life meet up since Grace was born. Teeny joined us. She was no longer stripping and now lived on a boat in Marina del Rey with her very nice boyfriend, named Eddie, who did something with computer programming.

We saw them all enter the park, and outwardly, not a thing had changed since the first time we'd met, except that Grace was no longer inside Bridgett. Bridgett and Bill were still all lanky limbs in blue jeans, long brown hair, matching black-and-neon-green Monster Energy drink T-shirts.

Bridgett, who had read on a Facebook post that I was looking for a new white cake recipe because I had failed miserably on my last attempt, handed me an angel-food cake recipe that she'd printed out from the Internet. It used Splenda instead of sugar. She'd carefully encased it in a clear plastic page protector and stuffed in some coupons for some of the ingredients.

I gave her a framed picture of Grace.

Reintroducing your kid to her birth parents isn't a situation most parents face, to be sure. It wasn't weird for Grace, of course, because all she really cared about was getting pushed on the swing and figuring out inventive new ways to go down the slide. But it was weird for all the adults—especially for Bridgett, who is shy to initiate conversations; Bill, who talked a lot about the big dreams of the past and future; and Peter, who seemed uncomfortable with the whole idea of another set of parents. I was actually glad to have Teeny there; she was kind of like a fairy-tale godmother who had a connection to Grace but no major stakes involved. We discussed a book Bill wrote, called *The Final Addendum*, described, in part, as: "The approach to the creation event with mathematical correlations in Bible observations, based on its accurate connection with real historical events." I imagined Bill's brain, in gear like a Rube Goldberg machine, constantly flooded by a tidal wave of thoughts. Whenever I don't know what to say, I usually let out a "huh," a nonjudgmental signal for "tell me more."

"Huh," I said.

Bridgett told me her idea for a hot-plate/microwave cookbook geared for people who had limited cooking space and resources, such as those living in dorms, and I thought it was excellent. I offered to help her put it together if she typed it. I never saw it after that.

Conversations stopped short every time Grace discovered an escape route from the playground or took a spill. I was in prime secret-service mode, always scanning for the potential catastrophe while trying to let her experience the world on her own terms. Peter, not a great one for ice breaking in the most normal of situations, wore a pained expression and kept the conversation mostly about music and his time as a rocker.

Bridgett and Bill seemed curious about Grace and amused by her, but kept their adoration at a distance. There was no smothering, no ebullient tickling, no obvious tears of, well, anything. I tried to give them as much space together as possible. At one point, Bill helped Grace up on one of those cars with a giant spring under it that made it sway and bounce. Out of nowhere, Grace gave Bill a kiss. It felt like a soul calling, a recognition. A punctuation mark.

We met up again for short visits. Once, in a park near our house, Bill, Bridgett, and I laid out a picnic while Grace perfected the art of climbing up a slide. Bridgett's Blackberry buzzed—it was a rare call from her mother. They talked a little, and then she handed the phone to me to say hi. I was introduced as a friend—the family still hadn't been let in on the pregnancy, let alone the adoption.

"Hi," I said. "It's Vanessa."

"Hi, you all having fun?"

The voice on the end was warm and craggy, its melody ravaged by time and maybe cigarettes and who knows what other kinds of hard living.

"Tell me about when Bridgett was little," I said.

"She was the cutest little girl you ever saw. She had these curly pigtails. I used to put them up with ribbons."

There wasn't much more to go on from there, but Bridgett's mother pronounced that I was nice, and she promised to come to LA to visit. I said I'd love to meet her. And I meant that: I was starving to know more. I am intensely curious every day about Grace's original kin, and I have always wanted to unearth the mystery that is Bridgett. The more DNA I understand, the better I will know my daughter. And the better I can help her to know herself.

Twelve

A Marriage Unravels

Since we'd become a pack of three, there hadn't been much alone time together for Peter and me as a married couple. And maybe that was part of the problem. My resentments were slowly, imperceptibly building. Peter was still paying debts and alimony from his previous marriage and contributed funds for our utilities, groceries, and dinners out. I was shouldering most of the financial burdens of our life, paying the mortgage, managing the rental property I owned, acting as activities director. I'd signed up for this. I thought marriage would be a protective shield against everything negative. But my optimism would prove to be a liar.

I was struggling for my own financial and career survival. I thought there'd be a magical safety net in marriage, but there wasn't.

My job had become unbearably toxic with another management switch—I'd been on top of my game under the old regime, but the new manager questioned my capacity and judgment at every turn, until I became an anxious wreck. I was one of the social-media pioneers in our industry, training executives, customer-service people, and communicators. I knew what I was doing. At one point, I used a relevant hashtag, #stoprush, on Twitter to respond in the conversation with people who wanted us to pull advertising from the *Rush Limbaugh Show*. The rest of the tweet was verbatim from my manager, that we'd review our advertising options. I was shocked and completely unsettled when I was called into a meeting with HR after being "thrown under the bus" by my manager, as they say in corporate land, for adding the hashtag. I was given an indefinite suspension and every day wondered if I'd get the call from HR saying that I could come back to work or that I was fired. After three weeks of wondering if I had a job, I was summoned back to work and given two weeks' pay because they couldn't really find anything wrong with what I'd done. I still feel mad that they bullied me out of the other week's salary.

I cried my way to and from work because it had become so unpredictable, so hostile feeling to a mama with a young child. At one point the company offered some workers a buyout that would have paid me four months' salary, $10,000 worth of education, and unemployment. I wanted the kind of husband who would say, "Take the deal. I've got this." But Peter wasn't that guy. He was scared we wouldn't be able to swing it. I reluctantly put on my misses career separates each day and drove to work—Peter would go in early and I'd go in later so that Grace wouldn't have to be at day care for such a long time. I got a prescription for antianxiety meds. The lorazepam, which I was supposed to take before work, sleep, and any time I was faced with an anxiety-provoking situation, such as a meeting with my manager, made me feel dull and uncreative. But even worse, it stole my dreams. Literally, as in, I stopped dreaming at night, which is a problem for me because I use my dreams as a way to get hints from my subconscious about my deeper inner life. My dreams give me important messages, like the ones telling me I'd find my daughter.

There's almost nothing as important as understanding your own self, but in the days of my corporate life, it felt like getting to work without being in shambles—rather than imploding in an unprofessional mess—was the more acute mission. I needed that job.

Peter was supportive, in his own way. He was always himself—stable and predictable. Every day after work, he'd change into his cargo shorts, T-shirt, and sneakers and pour a glass of wine and sit in front of the TV. Sometimes he'd pick up the guitar, and once in a while he'd gig when friends invited him to front a band, but he had no ambition to restart his own music career or go to a different job. Not at fifty years old. Not with a little kid. But his fear of me leaving work made me understand on a deeply visceral level that, really, we were two people journeying in two separate cars on the same road. I'd thought somehow it would be different. That we'd be propping each other up, taking turns, evolving together. That marriage would make us greater than the sum of him plus me. Peter is not a visionary. He doesn't have big dreams and, in fact, nicknamed our marriage "our little life," which felt warm and sweet at the time but didn't leave room for risk taking.

That spring was unremarkable, mostly, except for the one day I went to lunch with a colleague at a ramen place. That afternoon, I felt queasy and left work early and came home, doubling over with stomach cramps. As I sat on the toilet, projectile shitting out whatever universe of foul matter was inside me, I also had to throw up, so I grabbed the little trash can by the toilet. Grace was about a year old, still crawling but not yet walking, and I needed Peter to take over as I scooted the ten feet from the only bathroom to our bedroom.

Peter, concerned, held Grace. I tried to muster a sloppy smile and crawled into bed. Grace, then, with zero warning, threw up the mashed banana she'd just eaten all over the pillow and went back to being her chirpy little self, with anything toxic completely eliminated. I realized I wasn't done with my evacuation and bolted back to the toilet. Grace's puke on the pillowcase would be a distant number three on my priority list at the moment.

And then, from the other room: "Vanessa, when are you going to be done? I have to get in there," Peter pleaded, a note of unusual urgency in his voice. I got off the toilet. Peter charged to the toilet just in time to take his turn throwing up—the bug had made its way to him in just a matter of moments.

But I wasn't quite done. "I have to shit! I have to shit!" I yelled. Peter had turned pale and clammy and was now sitting on the toilet.

"I'm sorry, I can't . . . ," he started. He didn't need to finish that sentence.

In a fit of desperation, I went into the kitchen, grabbed a large stewpot Vito had left behind, sat on it, and emptied more of the poison brew within.

Grace, meanwhile, was crawling around on the floor; Peter and I each kept half an eye on her to make sure she didn't get into anything unsafe. When it seemed that my floods had ebbed, I crawled into bed again, barely able to lift my head. I tried to convince Grace it was sleeping time, but she'd already had her regular ten a.m. and one p.m. naps at day care and wasn't fooled for a second that it was time to go down.

I heard a loud crash and groan. Peter had gotten up and fallen right over, like a mighty tree; his pants were still around his ankles. He'd passed out cold in the hallway between the bathroom and the bedroom. I jumped up and shook his shoulders. "Peter! Peter!" I panicked. He opened his eyes after a few long moments, and blood began to pour from his nose. We both got back in bed.

I called two neighbors to see if they could watch Grace. Neither answered. Peter was unable to even lift his head.

I needed to improvise. I'd read dozens of parenting books by this point, and not one of them had a chapter called, "What to Do When You and Your Husband Are Crapping and Puking Black Death and You Can't Take Care of Your Child."

I got a cardboard box and put Grace inside with a book and a slice of bread, and she sat there, occupied, for a good twenty-five minutes. One of the neighbors called me back and was finally able to take her for a few hours so we could get some sleep.

It wasn't Peter's fault he got sick—I'd been the one to import the bug into our home from the ramen place, I was certain of this. But I wanted him to take over, to call in the cavalry, to fix it all. Of course he couldn't; he was human, only a man with his own biology. But these tiny few hours of our lives made it clear to me that nobody would be able to carry me, ever. I'd have to always figure it out on my own.

I also can't fault Peter for any kind of change that led to our relationship's slow implosion. We'd not had one fight since I stopped drinking early on in the marriage. The realization that I needed to be sober had come for me, hard and heavy, when I'd gone out for drinks with colleagues after work. I'd had about two glasses of wine, nibbled on some appetizers, and then got halfway through another glass of wine before I left.

I drove home and sat at the computer to type an email. Which I couldn't do. I lacked the coordination to form even a complete sentence. And I thought, in horror, that it was only dumb-ass luck that I'd been able to drive the seven miles back without incident.

I'd anticipated what marriage would be like—the comforting banality of it, the solid kind of smugness that came with being part of a family—but what I hadn't expected was a swath of secrecy that tore through our relationship.

If you plotted the highs and lows of our marriage on a graph, you'd start it high up, at the engagement. The line would ascend to the wedding, and then go up even farther when we became parents. And then you'd notice a new downward trend on one Saturday night around Christmas, when Grace was six months old. I'd dressed her in a fancy deep-emerald taffeta party dress and myself in a grass-green vintage lace dress for two parties we'd been invited to: one at Peter's friends' in his old Chino Hills neighborhood, about forty-five minutes away; the other at Sanjiv, Kaumudi, and Keya's, across the driveway. The plan was to hit the far-away one first. About six p.m., we got in Peter's truck, Grace tucked away in her seat in the back, me in the passenger seat. Peter eased out from our neighborhood roads to the highway. Then the truck veered around State Route 134, cutting across lanes. Peter overcorrected, jutting back to the right lane, nearly landing us on the shoulder. A few feet down the road, we would have been meeting merging traffic.

"Have you been drinking?" I asked, petrified, my heart on fire, the truck barreling on.

"Maybe a little," Peter said sheepishly. "I'm OK, I can still drive."

"Pull over. Pull the fuck over right now," I demanded.

He did, finally, after some weak protests. I got in the driver's seat and drove us home in stony silence, my anger silently unfurling inside. No way were we going to that party.

We got back, and I scooped up Grace in her fancy little dress and held her close to me. Seething, I told Peter: "Stay here. Do not try to follow me."

I bundled up the baby and brought her next door to Kaumudi and Sanjiv's party, where I sat on the couch, clutching Grace, trying to comprehend all the things that could have happened on that ride, but didn't. I made small talk with other guests, and Grace served as a sufficient distraction.

A few minutes later, Peter knocked on the door. Like he was the regular old neighbor coming to the party. Like he hadn't nearly killed us all. I recoiled silently in the small apartment crowded with holiday revelers cooing over my baby—my perfect, beautiful baby, who was still OK.

I couldn't state the intensity of Peter's drinking. Maybe I noticed it only after I took a break and became sober; maybe it was all my imagination, as he insisted. He didn't become anything radically different when he drank, loud or belligerent or funny or weepy, so I'd never noticed too much.

But my trust continued to erode. A couple weeks after the Christmas incident, I came home from work in the afternoon to an empty chardonnay bottle that had been half full the night before. It could have been consumed only between the time he came home and left again to pick Grace up from day care. I asked him about it and he denied it, as if he'd not been near a bottle in one hundred years. I wanted to believe him, and so I did.

Most nights, I would smell cigarettes on his breath as we kissed good night, and I'd ask if he'd been smoking. He'd say no, every time. And every time I wanted to believe him, so I concocted a theory that because he'd been a smoker ages ago, there was still some residue in his lungs that would take years to expel, and it happened little by little. I would much rather have heard, "Yes, I'm an adult, I smoke, get over it," from him than the daily lie—a neighbor would later tell me she saw Peter smoking every afternoon out in our carport before I got home.

We'd have serious talks, and sometimes he was remorseful and promised to do better in aspects concerning his health. I'd make him repeat back to me what I said about how scared I was and how I wanted him to get help. In my family the women have always been the heart police—they oversee the men's food and nag them about exercise, hoping to squeeze out a few more good years before or after a stroke or other health threat. The men all die earlier anyway.

We went to counseling, where an old, counterculture hippie dude named Brian would sit back in his leather chair and tell us that in order to heal our relationship, we'd have to reestablish trust by sitting on the couch and talking about our feelings for twenty minutes every day. We tried this for about a week. Feelings were feelings. It didn't matter that much—no confession could save us. Our marriage felt like a closed circuit with no new energy coming in—Peter hardly went anywhere on his own volition, except to the garden plot he'd leased through the city. Eventually we didn't have anything to talk about. Brian told us, "I don't really see how I can help you." And we stopped going.

My resentments helped fuel the breakup. I'd carried an irrational envy of Peter's ex-wife—actually, all ex-wives who got alimony, or support during their marriage that allowed them to stay home. Even though I'd gone into the relationship with eyes wide open, I'd hoped that eventually Peter would be more of an equal financial partner, instead of continuing to be the breadwinner in his old marriage. There were no other wagons to hitch mine with. I was unable to let anything around work or parenting or my home slide, or it would all fall like a nearly dead tree that needed just one good storm to topple it.

Once, Peter had an idea I found ludicrous, bordering on repulsive.

"You should sell your property," he said.

I didn't think I heard him right. We were smack in the middle of the housing crisis.

"Oh, that's impossible. It's underwater now. If I sold, we'd have nothing. At least this way we have something."

The markets had tanked, and home values in Southern California were scraping whatever is under rock bottom. Molten lava, maybe.

"Maybe we could move to a place in Long Beach."

Long Beach was nearer to his family. I wouldn't have minded renting something there. "How about this: I'll rent out my place if you find a way to move us to Long Beach."

We halfheartedly looked for homes but never made a move. To be sure, we were cramped in my apartment—all available floor and wall space was taken by the few things Peter had kept from his last home, plus whatever I had from before. But I also suspected that it would have been easier for Peter if we'd both had nothing, together.

The day before Grace's second birthday, the three of us were on vacation, staying with my cousins in their grand, old townhome in downtown Portland, Maine. After days of romping around on beaches and attending big family dinners, Cousin Elizabeth kindly offered to babysit so that Peter and I could go out on our own. We hit a bustling boutique ramen place for dinner and then meandered down the cobbled New England streets on that balmy summer night to a movie house.

We bought two tickets for *Now You See Me*, a film about a group of talented young grifters and illusionists who come together to help an old con, played by Michael Caine, do that huge, last-hurrah heist. We had time to kill before our show and stepped into a nearly empty Starbucks.

"I want to have a hard conversation with you," said Peter, looking at me across a small table, our coffees untouched. "There's something I need from you. The word is . . ." He searched; he paused. "Affection. I'm not getting any affection from you."

I'd known this was going to come down, eventually. He was good at being married—seventeen years at the last stretch. He understood the ebbs and flows of sticking out a relationship. He had been at the same job for more than twenty-five years. He was the embodiment of the law of motion, the one that illuminates how bodies at rest stay at rest. He knew how to stay in one place.

I wasn't wired the same way. I wanted to be married and thought, on the day, that we'd sealed the deal forever. Growing up in a single-dad household, though, I didn't have the training for marriage. It was kind of a dirty word, an antiquated concept. I didn't understand how to navigate the chasm between what I thought marriage would be like and its reality. In my mind I thought that we'd keep going deeper with each other, that we'd grow closer and better and more evolved as individuals and as a couple. But I didn't see that happening. I got the man I married, and he got me. It wasn't so much that we changed; it was more like the veneer got scratched off, and as each layer revealed more, we needed to reckon if we could still live with that person—was the bond stronger or weaker with every layer exposed? As badly as I wanted to be a family, and as ashamed as I was to see that I'd failed as a wife so quickly, in less than three years, I couldn't rise to meet the challenge.

Affection. We still held hands and kissed goodbye and hello, bookends to our comings and goings. But he was right. I couldn't go deeper. I'd lost that loving feeling. In that thick moment over coffee and milk and sugar, my answer would determine the future of our family. I couldn't recover from little and big breaches of trust. There was no turning back from the Christmas party night when he'd driven us, swerving, all over the road.

In that Starbucks, on that very last date we'd go on as a couple, I told him what had been brewing inside. I knew, logically, that you were supposed to get through anything with your spouse—that was the "in sickness and in health" part. But what if the sickness never got better?

I didn't see him making any meaningful moves to mitigate the drinking—he didn't believe he had a problem. I thought he did and it would kill one or all of us. I don't know what would have happened if he'd stopped, or even acknowledged his behavior. I'd like to think that we would have made it.

"I can't get back to the place I need to be, not after everything that happened," I admitted. It sounded like a surprise, even to me.

My tongue stuck in my throat. My mind briefly tried to stitch together a scenario in which we could still live together and raise our daughter. He would be having knee surgery soon, and I still wanted to be a Wife with a capital *W* for that. But at this moment, we were irreparably split.

Peter got up and shook my hand. "Thanks for letting me know. I guess we'll get divorced now."

He left the coffee shop and headed out into the cool safety of Portland's night streets. I sat for a few moments, stunned.

The movie tickets burned a hole in my pocket. And because I didn't know what else to do, I used one, returned the other, and watched the film. I walked home slowly, dreading whatever would come next. The rooms in my cousin's sprawling home were small and the walls thin enough that I could hear Peter mutter in anguish all night in the room next to the one Grace and I slept in: "Cunt," he said. "That fucking cunt." Over and over again. I got it. He'd been broken, and not even in the comfort of his own home. I'd be rageful, too.

The rest of the vacation was, as expected, strained. I told my cousins what had happened, and we all tried to act as normally as possible, which, of course, was impossible. A ticket change for Peter to go back early would have cost nearly $1,000, so we suffered through an impromptu second birthday party for Grace the next day. Peter played guitar, and Grace, her cousin Mary, and some little neighbor girls played like it was any other party.

I worried what Bridgett and Bill would think about the divorce. I knew that generally birth parents wanted the baby to go to a home with a two-parent family. Part of the reason Bridgett and Bill switched from the single woman on deck to adopt Grace before us was because she was too busy to even help Bridgett to the doctor; would she have been too busy for the child? How would they feel about me as a single mom?

When I broke the news of the divorce to them, assuring them that the split was amicable and that Peter would live close by, they were immediately supportive. Almost too supportive, like maybe they'd been expecting something like this. I knew they liked Peter, and I'd always suspected that his being a musician was the thing that clinched their initial interest in us as parents.

Bill wrote back immediately. He was supportive of the split, without taking sides or asking questions, and even suggested minimal visitation and custody. "It would not be unreasonable for Peter to relinquish all rights as Grace will not remember much about all this if it never becomes a custody [battle] that will scar her for the rest of her life." Bridgett chimed in, saying that she was sad about it but understood and that she hoped it would go smoothly for all involved. "We know Gracie is in good hands with you . . . You're a good person and he can trust you just as we trust you." And then she added a kitty-cat punctuation emoji at the end.

It wasn't that I didn't want Peter to raise Grace. They had their own relationship, and I thought—I still do—that it was incredibly important for them to be close. I just didn't want her to grow up in a home where people weren't loving on each other. I told him how terrible it would be for Grace to smell the omnipresent day-old booze seeping from his pores, because I didn't want her, in her later years, to be attracted to heavy drinkers. What I didn't know was how to fully absorb our schism—I thought drinking was the problem, its symptom, and its by-product of our split. He steadfastly denied there was an issue.

I wanted to be supportive, though, and invited him to stay in my apartment as long as he needed to after his upcoming knee-replacement surgery. He agreed. He would stay until he was healed, and then he'd look for a place nearby.

I worried about Grace adjusting. But maybe I shouldn't have, if how she quit her bottle just before she turned two was any indication. She had been so addicted to it, like in a junkie kind of way. Writhing and screaming if she didn't get it, ready to do physical damage to anyone who stood in the way of her "milt."

The final shattering glass and splattering milk happened on the shiny marble hotel floor in San Diego, the end of an epoch. I looked for signs of her freaking out and then took a picture of the mess before the bellmen scurried around to clean it up.

"OK, Grace," I explained after shoving several bills at the workers and apologizing profusely, as I had done exactly eleven times before, because usually the broken bottles occurred on hard restaurant floors or the concrete sidewalks under outdoor tables. "The last bottle is broken. Bottles are for babies, and you're a big girl now. No more bottle. Say bye-bye to ba-ba."

"Ba-ba broken," she repeated over the next few days, sometimes as a statement, sometimes as a question.

I had expected gnashing of teeth and wailing. But it never came. And the "ba-ba broken?" question eventually came every other day, then every few weeks, and then not at all.

Instead, the transition was flawless and kind of beautiful, and I got a better understanding of how Grace processed change. She lived up to her name as she navigated our new family dynamic. She didn't act out. She rolled with it all and loved us both.

A couple weeks after our decision to split, Peter was still in the house, recovering from knee-replacement surgery. I hoped he would stay until he healed up, and I wanted to take care of his basic needs. But he was antsy. When there was a new bottle of Gatorade in the fridge, I knew he'd gone out to get it. The nearest store was a ten-minute walk away on regular legs, and he'd never even done that without my urging.

"Hey, I see you went out to the store. How did you get there?"

"I drove. I needed to get out of the house," he said.

"Well, just don't. I'll get you whatever you want. Just tell me and I'll bring it home for you. I don't want you driving on painkillers."

A couple days later, on a hot July afternoon, when I'd returned from work, Peter still on the couch recovering, I stepped out to walk the dogs. As I approached the sidewalk, a cop in uniform stopped me and asked me if Peter lived here.

"Why?" I asked.

"Do you know if he was involved in a hit-and-run accident today? Someone saw him hit a parked car and drive away."

My blood turned icy.

"I don't know. Let's go find out."

I led him back to our apartment, where Peter was in his usual pose, spread out on the couch, his bum leg splayed out in front of him.

"Sir, were you involved in a hit-and-run accident today?" the cop asked.

"Naw, there must be some mistake," Peter said, turning his blue eyes onto the Power Mesmerize setting.

"That's interesting. Someone saw you do that, and the marks on your truck seem to be consistent with the damage to the car that was hit," said the cop.

Then Peter shifted into dude-bro sympathy mode. "Hey, man, my leg . . . can't you see?"

I watched their exchange, hoping that the officer wouldn't fall for it. Maybe a scare like this was the thing Peter would need. The son of a cop himself, he'd gotten out of more than a few scrapes just by dropping that knowledge and from having a special license-plate frame that indicated he was "in the family."

"Sir, I can see from your eyes that you're high. Have you been taking painkillers? We can do this the easy way or the hard way. Luckily, the party you hit is willing to not press charges if you can go through your insurance company and fix the car. Or we can do it the hard way, and I'll write you up right now for a misdemeanor."

"I'll do the insurance," Peter said sheepishly. I walked out to his truck with the officer and fished out Peter's insurance information from the glove box.

That night, I gave Peter two options.

"You can call your health insurance and get some help. You need treatment," I said. "Or you can move out next week."

I thought that it was an easy choice: just make the one phone call and go through the motions to appease me. He could have even negotiated down to attending an AA meeting and I would have been fine with it.

"I can't believe you're kicking me out," he said. He didn't believe he needed any kind of treatment, so he saw only one option.

"I'm not; you have a choice. Just go get some help, and you don't have to leave," I told him.

We had this exact conversation about a dozen times, each without him ever recognizing that treatment was on the table as a way to stay at home until he had healed.

A few months later, the preschool called me and told me that they were hesitant to release Grace to him because he stank to the high skies of booze, and they thought he might have been drinking. They assessed that he wasn't actually drunk but warned that next time, if they couldn't find me, it would be a call to Child Protective Services.

Peter moved a few blocks away, and we tried to keep doing things together as a family because we thought it would be good for Grace. But during the first experimental post–nuclear family dinner together, over small talk and calamari, Peter started to interject "fuck you" to me over and over, apropos of nothing.

As in, I would say something like, "So Grace has been making her own sandwiches; it's really cute. Soy nut butter."

"Fuck you."

"Do you mind?" I was horrified that Grace would think this was how normal people had conversations. Then changing the subject: "What are your girls up to?"

"Fuck you."

The restaurant was a short drive from our neighborhood, but on the way home, he kept badgering me about being a "quitter." I asked him to stop—I didn't want Grace to witness this dynamic between us and the staccato cursing from her dad. He didn't stop. Finally, I had to pull over and order him out of the car and leave him on the sidewalk, about a twenty-minute trek to his apartment. His knee had healed by this point. I'd hoped to make the transition from married to divorced as loving and as smooth as possible. But sometimes even the most conscious and earnest efforts to feel like a family failed.

We told Grace she had two homes, one with Mama and one with Dada. She asked a lot in the beginning, "Where's Dada? Is he sleeping at his house?" She also developed a mantra: "Dada's OK. Gracie's OK. Mama's OK." And she talked a lot about home when she was with me: "Gracie's home," as she knew my place was hers, too.

One night, when Peter came over in an attempt to be our new version of family, Grace was eager to get in the bath after drawing on her feet with red Magic Markers. As she pulled off her diaper, she banged her head on the tub and started crying. Still sniffling, she got in the bath long enough to wash the marker off her feet, which was about forty seconds, and then wanted to get out. I covered her in a towel, picked her up, and she started wailing again, wrapping her soapy little body tight around me. She wouldn't let me put her down and directed me to get her some milk and her blanket. And she cried some more, from a deeper place inside her than a head bump (I'm her mama; I decode cries like a bird-watcher can tell the subtle variation between an American robin's dawn and daytime calls).

And then she asked for "Mama night-night" and "Dada night-night," which meant she wanted both of us to come lie down and read to her and snuggle until she went to sleep.

So each of us lay down on either side of her in my queen bed, and Peter read a story, and I just breathed in soapy, clean little girl smell. After the book I turned out the light, and the room took on a low, fiery glow from the last of the daylight fighting through the orange shantung silk curtains I'd made and hung after Peter had left. Grace took each of our hands and tried to connect us.

Once, a girlfriend came with me to pick up Grace from Peter's on a Saturday afternoon. She gave him a hug and recoiled from the alcohol stench. It was a tipping point for me—another person had corroborated what I'd suspected. I freaked, filled out some paperwork, and headed to the courthouse with the intent of getting an order for him to get treatment. Peter brought along his attorney. I sat waiting, behind them, alone. The judge did not take my fear seriously. "Neither party can drink for four hours before getting in a car," he said. As if I were the one showing up hungover.

We'd switched day cares when the first mom-and-pop couple began to have health issues and worried that they wouldn't be able to do their best with the children, and my next-door neighbor, Valentin, didn't miss a beat in offering to watch Grace—as well as the other kids—every day. She loved Grace like a daughter and called her "my angel" and fed her all the rice and cookies she could eat. But when Grace was about two and a half, I realized the living room at Valentin's was just too small. Grace needed space and structure. She needed school. Happily, we found a preschool attached to an Episcopalian church one block away, where the religious education could best be described as "the Bible's greatest hits." The classes were small and the staff unfailingly attentive and kind.

Every day for a month prior to starting school, we'd pass by the mural featuring cheery pairs of animals embarking on Noah's ark. Grace would point and say, "My fool! My fool!" (She had trouble pronouncing her *s* still.) She was excited about her new preschool, mostly because it had a playground.

The morning of her first day, I asked if she was ready to go to school. "No. I want to go to the other playground," she said defiantly.

She was alternately fussy and exuberant, eating only a few bites of her scrambled egg.

Watching me pack her lunch, she carefully selected a blueberry yogurt and put it in the new, insulated Hello Kitty lunch box, purchased during a special trip to Chinatown for this very occasion.

She posed for a picture in front of the school's yellow banner, her wild curls in a halo, wearing a pretty blue-and-white floral cotton top. We got there early so she could meet her teacher. She played with small plastic cows, Play-Doh, and a spatula. She handed another girl in her class a Lego and called it a robot.

It looked like they'd be friends.

Then I told her I had to leave for work, and she cried. Fat, salty tears bumped down her perfect pink cheeks. "I wanna go to work! I wanna go to work!" she said as she clung to my neck as if it were a buoy, like she would drown in a cold, dark sea if she let go.

I peeled her off and handed her to a woman I had known for exactly thirty-five minutes.

Grace wailed as I walked past the sandpit and out the gate. I hid behind a wall. For what, five, ten minutes? Grace used a year's worth of breath to scream her displeasure.

When she finally stopped, I peeked in through the gate. She was sitting on a stoop, alone, huffing on the green-and-pink butterfly blanket her grandmother had made her, a self-comfort tactic she had developed early on for going to sleep and for handling moments of anxiety. She watched forlornly as other kids played in the sand. I know it's my job as a parent to prep her to be independent, to move throughout the world on her own. But on that day, I would have traded it all to be a stay-at-home mom.

For most of my time on earth, I've kept a tally of what's going well in my life versus what's not. After failing at marriage, having painful goodbyes with my child each morning, and trekking on such tenuous territory at work, my balance sheet was blazing red. Wasn't there any one tiny, goddamn thing I could do right?

Thirteen

BRIDGETT AND BILL MOVE IN

For an imperfect storm of reasons, Bill and Bridgett became homeless in October of 2013. They said their apartment had become infested with bedbugs, and so they were holding back rent. There was also something about their landlord keeping their mail from them. Bridgett had been trying unsuccessfully to get a job at a supermarket or fast-food joint. She'd been close a few times but never was able to secure a gig. After Bill had worked many years for Pizza Hut franchises in Texas and Los Angeles as an assistant manager, an ownership change brought Bill back to near minimum wage. Then something about forgetting to issue a receipt to a customer, and bam, he was fired, he said. There was no money to put down a security deposit on another place—and who would accept these two jobless folks with a pet bunny anyway? What money they did get they'd made from royalties on "Hey Baby Que Paso," the song he cowrote, playing music at the Third Street Promenade in Santa Monica, as well as gigging at a small hotel lounge. They went through a revolving cast of untrained female drummers—basically friends they met—which didn't help their show prospects or continuity.

They were certain they'd get housed soon and somehow qualify for assistance with a small apartment. Bridgett and Bill did have enough to get a storage unit, into which they managed to move all their belongings. And then they bunked in a downtown homeless shelter. That didn't last long. First, it was crowded, and they had to physically show up to secure their spot for the night, then get lost for a few hours, and then show up on time in the evening (but not too late or the doors would close and they'd be left out in the street). Showers were allowed at arbitrary times. You couldn't leave anything there, which made going out and looking for work impossible—who wants to show up for a job interview with their whole life in a shopping cart? Not a good look. Nights were loud, and the other denizens weren't nice to them. Worst of all, Bill and Bridgett were separated at night into men's and women's quarters. That was, for them, the most unbearable part of it. Like characters out of a Capra movie, as much as they didn't have worldly goods and networks, they had each other, wrapped in impeccable loyalty and unquestioning commitment. Adversity tears some couples to shreds, but in this case, it was the adhesive they needed to keep it all moving forward. Their relationship was thicker and stickier than any I'd ever had.

Bill tried to exercise his status as a veteran, with mixed success. He filled out reams of paperwork for free housing in Los Angeles, but, he says, he was given only promises. There was little to no money coming in. He and Bridgett had given up on finding jobs—and even if they did go to work, then they probably wouldn't qualify for all the help they could get if they had nothing. So they waited. They built a home of tarps and tents and whatever materials they could salvage from the street, while keeping a storage unit for their music gear and more treasured possessions. The bunny didn't seem to mind her new home.

They felt freer on that gritty patch downtown on Seventeenth Street, near the freeway, in a way, than they could have if they had been bound to a home and job. Time stopped. They could wake and roam and sleep as they chose. They didn't worry about money.

Their days were spent adventuring like early explorers, scavenging things from dumpsters and the sidewalk to sell: a box of new hairbrushes. Shoes. Old stereo components. And the cans, always the cans. Their royalties from "Hey Baby Que Paso" trickled down to about one hundred dollars a year ("That song is still a hit," he told me. And in a way, it is, after being used in the very occasional movie or show.) They brought in about $650 a month from cans, they said, enough to buy a nightly beer for Bill and a Monster drink for Bridgett and some meat from the *carnicería* nearby, and have a barbecue on a salvaged hibachi.

They'd share their bounty with their neighbors, most notably a crackhead named Steve, who would watch their stuff while they were out. Most days, though, they'd have to carry everything with them, including the bunny, Ynnub, in a soft carrying case. She was so inconspicuous nobody ever knew she was with them.

They quickly learned the rules of street living:

Never pick your spot under a bridge; that is too dangerous.

Best to find a spot that has morning shade; otherwise you roast, like in an oven. Your spot will never be too far from someone else's spot.

Never leave your tent unoccupied, even for ten minutes when it's raining. But rainy days are great because you don't have to tear down and can catch up on some sleep.

The library is great for staying out of the weather and getting things done, like checking email.

It's best to set up camp by nine p.m., and it takes about an hour. Never set up camp later than eleven p.m.

Don't mess with other people living in tents. "Most tent people are so gross," Bill said. But they weren't. They went to extreme lengths to stay clean and look like a couple college students, maybe, on an extracasual day.

Bridgett and Bill said they weren't scared, usually. They had some run-ins with a few people, but in the end, "Most of our stories show the good side of people," Bill said.

They kept their dreams of being musicians in mind, meeting with industry people when the opportunity arose, staying connected to the world with Bridgett's little netbook computer and their Blackberries, with free Wi-Fi from McDonald's or Starbucks or the library.

It was the week before Thanksgiving 2013, and Grace was nearly two and a half, and I invited Bill and Bridgett for dinner, an early celebration we could do as a kind of family. They said yes.

Grace and I met them at the train and spirited them home. I'd made a Thanksgiving-lite feast: half a turkey, cranberry sauce, sweet potatoes. A pie.

We sat around the table like four people at any dinner, except the conversation was about life on the street, why the shelter was an unthinkable option, what the hurdles were to getting VA housing. They finished every crumb from their plates, plus seconds and thirds. There were no leftovers.

The season's darkness and cold had descended on the neighborhood. I thought through the logistics of piling an increasingly sleepy Grace into the car as I brought them back downtown.

"Do you guys want to just stay over?"

"Sure."

"OK, well, make yourself comfortable," I told them.

They took a forty-five-minute shower together. Grace's first memory isn't of me or her dad or playing with cousins or a birthday party. This is her first memory, she says—them in the shower for what seemed, to her, like an eternity.

They slept in Grace's room while she bunked with me, and woke up late the next day and went back to the tent downtown. I gave them all our extra blankets and some DVDs they could watch on a small, battery-operated player Bridgett had procured from somewhere. There's a lot of time to pass when you're in a tent.

After our pre-Thanksgiving dinner, Grace drew a picture on our kitchen chalkboard in pink, two people with big, round interlocking heads and one stick-figure body. Ever since she was able to hold a pencil, her main artistic theme has been us together. Even after she expanded her repertoire to include bunnies, flowers, hearts, stars, and puppies, there was usually a drawing of her and me, and an "I love Mom" in there. She's for sure a mama's girl. At least for now.

I cooed over her drawing and asked her if it was us, assuming I knew the answer. "No," she said. "It's Bridgett and Bill." Apparently she couldn't stop thinking about them, either.

This would not be the first time her power of perception and metaphor would flatten me. She was so spot on with how they were two, but one. She got it. She came from that alchemy, so maybe I shouldn't have been so surprised.

The next week, it started raining. Pounding, pouring rain, flooding a city that is better suited to fielding the mad wrath of the sun and all that it brings. A serious rain in Los Angeles immobilizes the city. It reveals all its design flaws and carries away the grime and oil and regrets accumulated since the last rain. Monsoon season is the most dreadful time to be homeless in LA, maybe even worse than a sweltering summer.

The thought occurred that I should invite Bridgett and Bill to stay with me until the weather got better. But then I shooed it away like a pesky mosquito. Because, you know, boundaries. I was a single, working mother with no extra time, money, or energy. I got a pass, right? But then they occupied an uncomfortably large space in my brain. Something had shifted. Like a debt becoming obvious and, in a way, deeper. I just couldn't stop thinking about them, out there in the rain and cold.

Grace and I were good. Peter had been out of the house for six months. I took home a paycheck and never had trouble paying a bill. We were safe and warm in our two-bedroom, not-even-one-thousand-square-foot home. In comparison to, say, most people around the world, or a typical New Yorker, we were living in palatial splendor. Why shouldn't we share? Especially to the people who had given me the greatest gift?

I'm not a perpetual do-gooder. An uncomfortable proportion of my thoughts are impure and judgmental. When I was a kid, my UNICEF Halloween change found its way only to the closest candy store, never as far as the starving African children for which it was intended. I am impatient with my mother's endless ideas for my improvement. And I swear like a motherfucking carny on a bender. But I didn't think I could lie in my bed, my sweet, curly-haired girl sighing peacefully in her sleep next to me, without being haunted by the thought of Bill and Bridgett trying to keep warm and dry.

"Do you want to stay with us for a little while?" I asked Bill and Bridgett in a Facebook message.

They did.

And a few hours later, I was loading up my daughter's original parents into my 2006 Prius, along with Bill's guitar, Bridgett's bass, and a couple day bags.

This will either end really well or really badly, I thought, shutting the car doors. Jesus, what have I done?

Grace had become more fearless, crackerjack smart, always searching for more independence. She'd been alive only a week or two when she started holding her bottle on her own. "I can do it *myself*!" had become her mantra as soon as she could string together words. Today, though, she was terrified of Ynnub the bunny, the first she had ever seen outside of a book, as I gently wedged Ynnub's cage between her and Bridgett in the back seat.

In my mind they would stay until the rain stopped.

But we'd never had the actual discussion about expectations—theirs from me, mine from them, including how long they'd stay. The weather gods were on Bridgett and Bill's side, keeping our outside world cold and wet and miserable for weeks.

They needed everything. Bedbugs from their last apartment had decimated their wardrobes, they said. They shared a couple pairs of underwear. Whenever Bridgett laughed, she put her hand over her mouth to hide her left canine tooth, which had turned black. Bill needed glasses but didn't have them. Anytime he needed to really see something, he'd borrow Bridgett's—to this day I can't understand why they didn't go to the VA to get their teeth and eyes sorted. But in talking about our various eyesight issues, we figured out that we were all on the similarly bad spot of the nearsightedness spectrum, and my pair of green-framed, rectangular-rimmed glasses I'd thought were avant-garde when I bought them but really just looked insane on me sort of worked for Bill, so he took those. I found them a program through a national chain that helps people in need get exams and glasses, but they didn't follow up.

I reached out on their behalf, realizing that I couldn't get them everything on my own, and posted a message on Facebook: "Everyone, this year, instead of donating to charitable organizations, I'm focusing on the people I know who really, really need help. At this time, it happens to be my daughter's birth parents, who have recently become homeless. They are staying with us because it's freezing outside and because they're trying to get into the next place . . . If you're so inclined to give to people who can really use some help, I'm happy to help get anything to them. They are very shy about asking for things but had to leave most of their clothes when they left their last place. They don't need a lot of actual stuff, because they don't have anywhere to put it yet. Of course any gift cards are welcome; they tend to frequent the ninety-nine cents store and Goodwill and Target. If you want to send cash or check, let me know and you can send c/o me until they figure out their PayPal acct."

At the bottom, I added a list of things they needed and their sizes: A laptop. Shampoo and conditioner. Jeans. Underwear. It struck me that they were so thin the sizes they requested were for boys' and girls' large—not even men's and women's small.

Because people are so, so good, they helped. My cry for supplies amplified through my network, and the love multiplied. The generosity of my friends, and their friends and family, astounded me. For the next several days, the gifts started to pile up, including new underwear for Bridgett from a mom I'd just become friends with, who had just adopted a little boy from the foster system; designer lingerie, bras, jeans, and newish Uggs for Bridgett from my friend Joanna; a MacBook Pro that had been cleaned up and rebooted, from my friend Robin; gift cards for Trader Joe's and Macy's and even generic Visa cards from friends, acquaintances, and strangers; DVDs and food in a care package; pellets and timothy hay for the bunny. One friend of a not-even-close friend saw the post and sent a bunny cage from Michigan. The cost of postage was more than it would have been to buy a cage new. But sometimes people just want to do something, anything, to help. It was like an early Christmas. Every bag stuffed to the brim held the promise of functionality or beauty, something that would bring them closer to being normal people. Some of the stuff they didn't need or couldn't fit they planned to sell on Craigslist.

I was blown away. I couldn't tell if they were, too. But I know they like free stuff. They live for it. I compiled a meticulous list of everyone's address and email address and what they'd sent, and asked only one thing: that Bill and Bridgett send thank-you notes. They said "of course!" enthusiastically. I hope the people who donated still aren't waiting for those notes.

I found myself thinking hard about how I could solve more of their problems, besides clothes. I decided to put my game up a notch. Bill and Bridgett didn't just need things. They needed work. And systems. They needed to take advantage of all that was waiting out there in the world for them, resources they either didn't know about or just had not accessed.

What would I do if I were homeless?

Well, I chirpily answered myself, if I were homeless, I'd need a job!

I brought home a flyer calling for help at a local Starbucks. ("Starbucks is great! They have insurance! And will help pay for school, if you want!") They saw it and said thank you, never to mention it again.

Bridgett had grocery experience, and Bill had also worked in food, so it seemed natural to invite my friend Kathlyn, a manager at Trader Joe's, over on a sunny Saturday morning for a private tutorial on how to apply. We sat at the table, Kathlyn and I drinking tea, Bridgett sipping a Crystal Light. Bill slept in and missed the visit entirely.

"We like our employees to really love people. We want someone who is excited about the store's products and who enjoys working hard but also having fun—maybe even someone who thinks working hard is fun," Kathlyn said.

Bridgett nodded. Kathlyn continued.

"We'll always ask what your favorite Trader Joe's product is, so get ready for that question; maybe go take a look around the store and have it in your mind," Kathlyn said. "Mornings are the best time to approach the managers with an application. Find the captain at the store and see if you can get a word in. Visit as many stores as possible for a better chance."

Bridgett was quiet and didn't have many questions. She struck me as someone whose default was to just take what she was given. To not engage. Like speaking back would be a privilege she wasn't sure she had.

Kathlyn left without much faith that Bridgett would ever be hired there. She just seemed so shy, and like she'd never survive the fast and sometimes cutthroat culture behind the scenes.

In the days that followed, I questioned them about their job hunting. There was always a reason why they hadn't quite had time to start: They were busy working on housing stuff. It was too late to go in. Something. Anything. I stopped asking.

I'd recently made a career shift to work in philanthropy communications at a nonprofit health-care system. We provided free and low-cost care to those who needed it most through one of the largest medical charities in Southern California. My colleagues were hooked into public clinics and could expertly navigate the system. I told one manager about the plight of Bill and Bridgett, and he scrawled the phone number of the executive director of a clinic that could help with Bridgett's tooth and any other medical issues they were having. If they called, Bridgett and Bill wouldn't have to wait so long for an appointment—it could normally take months. I gave them the number and they seemed thankful. They said they called but never were able to connect.

They said they still needed jeans, so I gave them forty dollars to go to Goodwill, a fifteen-minute walk away. Not any rinky-dink shop. It was a huge, sprawling Goodwill, with what must have been five hundred pairs of jeans on the racks for the taking.

Bill and Bridgett set out walking and came back in what felt like record time, saying there were no jeans that fit, and instead, they had some groceries and beer from Trader Joe's. They handed me a small packet of dark-chocolate peanut-butter cups, because they knew I had a particular weakness for this confection.

Later, at three a.m., I woke up to the sticky-sweet, piney scent of weed. Nobody mentioned it the next day.

We developed a routine over those four weeks, a rhythm, as people do when they're together long enough.

I would get up, keep Grace as quiet as possible, so as not to wake our guests, and get her ready for preschool. Bill and Bridgett would get up around noon or later. I assumed they spent their days trying to hook into the VA housing, or look for jobs, or . . . something. Anything productive. And I guess there was some of that. But mostly, practicing music.

Bill and Bridgett moved quietly when I was home, as if they were trying to take up the least amount of space possible. I loaded the dishwasher, and Bridgett took each dish out and washed it by hand. They offered to babysit a couple times, which I accepted.

My inner control freak was starting to get twitchy, but I tried not to nag. After all, they were adults. And guests.

Still, I ended up asking every night what they were doing to move everything along. I wanted them to get it together. So that Grace would know she had come from strong, resilient stock. So that I didn't resent them for sleeping in while I ground out my forty-plus-hour workweek. So that they could do something else, anything, to make it seem like they were moving forward.

One night, I was trying to brush Grace's hair, a halo of golden curls. She resisted and tried to run away whenever I got near.

"Here, Grace, look," Bill said. He began brushing Bridgett's hair, long strokes down her back. "Doesn't that feel so good?"

They switched, and Bridgett started brushing Bill's hair. "Mmm! This feels great. Look how shiny!" they emphasized, for Grace's sake.

Grace stopped for a moment and watched them, and recoiled as they handed her the brush. She reminded me, in an oddly proud way, of the character Wolf in my all-time favorite movie, *Hair*. Wolf's steadfast and vocal refusal to let anyone shear his flaxen locks when he got to jail landed him in the shrink's office. Grace knew what she loved and didn't love. And in this way she was different than Bill and Bridgett, for now. Her hair was her own business.

The weather had started to improve. Though it dried out, it was still cold. How fair was fair? I started to wonder as I worried that they had no clear exit strategy. I wanted my home back the way it had been.

Even though in theory I am a proponent of the hard conversation— I know that the emotional work up front makes the rest of it easier—I was reluctant to have such a talk with Bill and Bridgett about how long they would stay and what I hoped their stay would accomplish. I didn't want to make them feel like they were putting me out, to send them back into the cold. I didn't want to be rude. So I settled for this: "Let's talk about your time here. It's not a vacation. I want you to be able to use this place, the computer, whatever you need to get your life back on track. So it makes me feel bad if I'm up at six a.m. and working a full day, and then you guys are up until three and sleeping in all day."

They understood. For the next week, they were quieter at night.

For cash, Bill and Bridgett collected cans from trash and recycling bins around town and stashed them neatly in a bag. But Grace's bedroom, where they were parked, was beginning to smell like an Irish pub at closing time, so I also got the courage to ask them to keep the cans somewhere else, outside. They hurriedly moved their bag of cans and bottles out to the parking area.

"Hey," they would say, daily. "We really appreciate your letting us stay here."

Every day I kept thinking that something magical would happen. A job. The VA housing. Something would come through.

Never, ever once did they give me the impression that they regretted their decision to make me Grace's mother. But still, one night when Grace thoroughly melted down into a puddle of snot and tears because she had to stop playing with the bunny and go to bed, I worried about having them in the front row of my parenting show. Would they still think I was a good mom?

I couldn't imagine what it was like for them to watch this magical little girl they created have a whole other family system, to sometimes not get a kiss good night from her, to not be able to just reach out and grab her and nuzzle their faces against her creamy skin. Which I guess they could have if they wanted to. But they kept a line. Grace also knew what side of the line she was on. She was sweet and friendly with them, a little shy, and always turned to me first for cuddles or help.

There was a seed of angst inside me that if they stayed too long, maybe Grace would have confusion about so many parents. It is the ultimate Darwinism to make sure your child is loved by many people. The more, the better. This was why, without discussion or deliberation, I wanted her to have her dad's last name—another connection to cement her into that family. I knew from all my adoption training and subsequent learning that the original separation wound is something that heals to various degrees in different people, but it is always there—I could never truly, entirely remove the scar Grace carries from growing inside one mother and being handed to another. But I spend every moment of every day wanting to be the biggest star in her life. The one who loves her the most. The one she loves the most. It is torture for me to imagine my life without her, or hers without me.

In mid-December there was a holiday breakfast at Grace's preschool. I'm pretty sure ours was the craziest picture Santa had that day—or maybe even ever. Bill and Bridgett were all hair. Peter came, too, holding crutches for his newly broken ankle, like some overgrown

Tiny Tim. Grace would have nothing to do with Santa, who was phoning it in, hoping the next kid wouldn't pee or puke on him, a yes-man to any wish whispered or shouted. I was stress smiling in a dumb, big red hat, trying to make it seem as if we were just one big, normal family.

After the photo op, we all sat down at a round table to eat pancakes off paper plates and drink bad church coffee out of Styrofoam cups. Grace stretched out her arms, wanting a lap. And of the four she could ask for, she climbed onto mine.

The days piled up and became weeks, and the weeks became more than a month that Bridgett and Bill were with us. I wondered what I could do to get some space—maybe they were also feeling the squeeze?—without asking them to just go back into the night. So just before Christmas, I put a call out to a neighborhood moms' group: "Do you need a house or pet sitter?" Someone did, an actress named Meaghan, while she and her toddler and husband went to France, starting Christmas Eve. They had a large dog that needed a lot of walks, and a cat. I told Meaghan the situation and assured her that I'd take responsibility in case anything went wrong. She, being a large-hearted sort, met Bill and Bridgett and gave them the key to her home, her life, for a full ten days. Bridgett and Bill left my home on Christmas Eve but came back the next day to spend Christmas with us.

On that day, Bridgett and I worked together to give Grace what I thought would be her most prized Christmas present. Grace had lost her teddy bear, Rainbow, the previous summer somewhere along the mile-long trek between home and the playground. It had been dark by the time we got back and realized the small pink teddy bear had fallen out of the stroller. The next morning I got up early and retraced our route, with no luck. Rainbow was gone. Every day for the next couple of weeks, she'd ask about Rainbow and I would always give the same answer: "Rainbow fell out of the stroller and is now living with another family. We probably won't see her anymore. I'm sorry, baby."

The inquiries grew further and further apart, but she would still ask about Rainbow's whereabouts. I felt helpless.

And then I got an idea: Rainbow would make an amazing Christmas comeback.

Grace has some irreplaceable items—notably, the green blanket her grandmother made and the teddy bears given to her by the adoption agency and the judge who did her finalization. Rainbow, however, was one of a million mass-produced bears, and I happened to find a duplicate online, for under five dollars. She would never know the difference.

I laid out the elements of the plan to Bridgett. Rainbow was to return Christmas Day, like some tiny pink Bing Crosby coming home from the war. There would be a scarf and perhaps a small satchel. Bridgett had the idea to write a letter, in her faint pencil cursive, from Santa, who hinted at Rainbow's adventures hopping in the forest with bunnies and jamming in a band with Hello Kitty. A very nice touch, I thought.

On December 25, as we were clearing up dishes, Bridgett distracted Grace while I made the backdoor handoff to the neighbor, who placed Rainbow and the letter at our front door and rang the bell.

"HMM, WHO COULD THAT BE? I WONDER WHO COULD BE HERE ON CHRISTMAS DAY?" I said, to great dramatic effect, perhaps with a touch too much Liza Minnelli.

We opened the door. Rainbow! It was Rainbow! Who had come back! Wasn't that amazing?

Grace eyed Rainbow warily for a moment, then scooped up the bear and gave her a quick hug and went about her business with the other toys she'd gotten that day. Bridgett and I locked eyes in a silent, secret high five. Mission accomplished.

Later that night, Grace asked me, "Mom, where's the other Rainbow?" I dodged by asking her other questions, completely thrown that she was onto us.

The next night, from the back seat of the car, she asked again, the bear on her lap. I turned around, sighed deeply, and told her the only thing I could think to say: "Baby, the other Rainbow fell out of the stroller, and we'll never see that one again. But this is a replacement Rainbow. I'm sorry. I couldn't find the other one."

She took Rainbow number two in her arms and gave it a bear hug, as much as a child in a car seat can. "That's OK," she said. "I like this one."

I was blown away by her capacity to absorb loss—I don't know why I'd underestimated her. In fact, everyone seemed to be absorbing loss so very well.

When Bridgett and Bill went off to house-sit for Meaghan, my place went back to normal, in that I didn't hear midnight scuffling and bumping. I didn't have to navigate around Bill's and Bridgett's presence, never more than a few feet away. I was able to pee with the bathroom door open again. I could breathe out, fully. Mostly.

In January, at the end of the ten-day house-sitting gig, Bridgett and Bill returned to our place. Meaghan reported that they'd left the place spotless and everything seemed fine. Which was a relief. I knew from living with them that they were trustworthy—I'd once found a twenty-dollar bill on the steps to my kitchen, which I'd thought might be theirs. They said no. It turned out to be mine, but it was a nice, accidental assurance that even though they were homeless, and destitute, and had no prospects, they were still good at their core.

But they were starting to feel caged in at my house and said they missed their adventuring life and wanted to be closer to the services—there was a chance they could get veterans' housing and wanted to pounce when the call came. So they left, back to their tent downtown. I was thankful that they'd made the call to leave and it wasn't up to me to ask them to go.

For the most part, they stayed downtown. Sometimes they'd miss the cutoff time at the shelter, and it would be too late to set up camp, and they'd ask if they could stay that night, and I always said yes. In early February there was the one late-night call from Bill. Something messy and scary going down in their neighborhood. What sounded like a gang rape. Possibly a murder, and their neighbor, Crackhead Steve, was missing. And they needed to disappear in case the perps were looking for witnesses to erase. And something about stolen speakers. They said they might be targets and needed to cool out here.

"Um, OK," I said. How could I not? My sister-friend Liza, whom I'd known my whole life, was visiting from Atlanta. We'd just settled into our chardonnay and movie night, with Grace asleep in my room. Liza was camped out in Grace's bed. "You'd have to sleep on the couch, though," I told them. That didn't deter them.

Liza and I had just begun watching *Philomena*, an Irish film, starring Judi Dench, about how the Catholic Church used to force girls and unmarried women to give up their babies for adoption to wealthy Americans and Brits, and enslave the mothers with laundry work for years after. Babies who didn't live were buried in unmarked graves on church land. It was another dirty Catholic secret that wreaked psychological havoc for generations. Probably not the best choice of film for that audience. Bridgett and Bill watched with us, quietly. I don't know why I didn't just turn it off and put on some dumb comedy instead. What compassionless, resentful, control-freak version of "If you're going to come here uninvited, you will have to do what we're doing even though it's ironically insensitive" compelled me to keep it on, I will never understand.

There were a few more drop-by overnights. And I understood; I always said yes. It's hard to plan things when you're homeless.

And then my girl started to change.

I don't know if Grace was piggybacking on my anxiety about the Bridgett and Bill situation. I'd been feeling unmoored, never knowing when the next call from them would be, never knowing if they were going to show up, never knowing if they were going to disappear for-ever. Or maybe Grace had her own issues she was working out—some primal abandonment issues—and was thrown by the uncertainty of it all. In her short two and a half years, she'd already had one new set of parents. Was there something deep seated in her that wondered if there was an expiration date on me?

Very suddenly, my normally chipper and sassy girl—who would usually go to bed with mild protests and repeat cycles of "Huggy! Cuddle!"—became afraid to go to sleep, in a dark, desperate way. She became afraid of shadows and light and the air without me in the room. The only way I could calm her was to hold her tight in my bed. And then, after a half hour or forty-five minutes, I'd try to sneak out, think-ing she was down, and she'd wail for me. She'd run to the couch, if I'd made it that far, and fling herself onto me. Once, she stayed up and watched an entire Steve Carell movie with me, way into the late hours, because she didn't want to go to sleep, and neither did I. This from a child who conquered sleeping alone in her crib at seven months old. From the girl who wanted to do everything herself.

"You're not their mom; you're Grace's mom," multiple people told me when they learned about Bridgett and Bill's plight and how I kept trying to change its course.

"Yeah, yeah, I got that," I said. But Bridgett and Bill had nobody. Not one person within a five-hundred-mile radius who would know, or care, if they were alive or dead. I had begun to rationalize that if I was a good kind of person, who could give fifty dollars to the Los Angeles Food Bank, I'd be an even better kind of person to give to homeless people whom I knew, where I could truly make a difference.

But maybe my friends were right. Maybe Peter was right to draw the line at "you can come over for a cookout" but not at "you can come stay here." He had clear boundaries. Easily defined. No complex knots to untie.

With Grace's newfound anxiety, I decided something needed to change, and the only denominator I could pinpoint was Bill and Bridgett's comings and goings. Not just for my own sake, but for my baby's.

And that was why, on the late Saturday night when they knocked on the door, it took me forever to answer it, and once I did, I couldn't let them in. And then they disconnected from me and disappeared.

Fourteen

Saying Hello Would Be a Terrible Idea

I'd shimmied into my sexiest low-cut black dress, an old thing that still did the job of announcing my décolletage but downplaying the tummy pooch. I'd hot rollered my hair like Marilyn Monroe, painted my eyes like Liz Taylor circa 1972, and finished the look with some black cat-eye glasses.

It was September of 2014, and I was driving to the premiere of a new television series, *Transparent*, at a theater downtown—if you live in LA for a while, someone will invariably invite you to something like this. Once I got downtown, two blocks from the theater, it turned into a logic puzzle to get there. All the traffic downtown had been rerouted into a slow-motion Escherian configuration: you couldn't get there from here. Nope, not this street, either. Try again. I was stopped on a side street, waiting for a light, wriggling my foot into a dangerously-high-heeled Michael Kors platform sandal, and I saw them for the first time, eight months since they'd left my doorstep.

Bill and Bridgett were less than ten feet from my car window. They were digging through a trash can for bottles and aluminum cans, making a living eight or ten cents at a time. They looked the same as always—long, smooth hair down their backs, jeans and T-shirts, gloves. Clean. Bill worked a grabbing tool to reach deep-down items; Bridgett minded a rolling cart. They looked absorbed in their work.

My breath stopped short. It had been almost a year since we'd had contact. I hadn't been sure if they'd actually gone to Texas or not. I froze like a possum in the road as I contemplated the best course. I couldn't take my eyes off them. If I said hello or waved, I would be catching them in a vulnerable moment. Would that be embarrassing to them? Would they even acknowledge me? If I didn't say hi, I would be snubbing the very people who gave life to my daughter.

So I did what came naturally: I ducked down under the dashboard and finished putting on my shoe.

When I sat back up, they were still picking cans. Either this was a freakishly long red light, or something had shifted in the time-space continuum. But in that drawn-out moment, I decided nothing positive would come from catching their attention. I thought that maybe if I could hide my eyes behind the rearview mirror, I would look like any other LA woman, big boobs in a black dress, driving a blue Prius.

They fished out their final bottle from the trash can, added it to the burgeoning bag, and walked on. My light changed and I drove forward. Ten minutes later I entered a building where the combined net worth of the people in it was in the hundreds of billions of dollars.

I thought about Bridgett and Bill all night, as I was jostling around paparazzi, pretending to be the publicist for a friend who wanted to walk the red carpet; as I clinked glasses in celebration of Jill Soloway's ground-breaking triumph of art and storytelling; as I drove home, fell asleep; and then for months afterward. I will never get that image of them scavenging out of my mind, nor will I ever be able to get over the great divide of who they are and who I am. I always wonder who Grace would be if they hadn't placed her with me, but then I always come back to the knowledge that her spirit is so strong and good that she would always be OK in this world. Even under the most adverse of circumstances. Everyone who has ever met her adores her instantly. I somehow take comfort in this.

Fifteen

Unfriended

I'd heard through the grapevine that Bridgett and Bill had finally headed off to Texas on a Greyhound bus, their bunny safely in a bag. Grace hadn't asked about them, but every day I felt the tug of unfinished business, the shame of not having done my best by them by not being clear in my expectations. The next-best course after a fumble is a correction, which I tried in an email to them.

> Dear Bill and Bridgett,
>
> I see that I've been unfriended and I'm hoping that you aren't mad at me. I know that your last few nights in Los Angeles didn't go very well, and it sounds like at least you're being helped in Texas, which eases my mind.
>
> You might be wondering why I didn't invite you to stay that last time you showed up at my door. I'm going to be heart-achingly honest here because I think that's the only way we can continue to have a good relationship.

I know you were scared to stay in your neighborhood, and you mentioned you were "targeted." I don't know the extent of this, but if there was even a hint of danger, I couldn't have you anywhere near our home. I know you'd never put Grace at risk on purpose, but I just couldn't take any chance that there could be something bad going down around her.

Also, I will say I was a little disappointed with how things worked out. I felt like in the end, I wanted different things than you wanted for yourself, and that's my mistake for assuming that I was being helpful by setting up job stuff, health-clinic contacts, etc. I was frustrated by your lack of timing and planning and serious job searching (I know that's a conundrum; if you're earning you might not be eligible for all the programs), and the one thing I asked, for thank-you notes to the people who gave you so much, never happened. It doesn't matter now. But it's my fault for assuming the same things that are important to me are important to you.

But the biggest reason I didn't invite you in is because it was stressing out Grace. I learn more about her every day, and I realize she needs to know what's happening in advance, whether it's a dentist appointment, washing her hair, or having people in our home. She needs to know how long and when and who, and she expressed, in her own way, that she wanted it to be just us for a while. I also felt that I wasn't being very helpful to you and that I needed to set some kind of boundary.

We love you and want you to win, and I know you will. Please keep us up on where you are and how you're doing.

I hope this note is received in the spirit it's intended, to tell family members the truth so that we can move forward with no resentments. If there's anything you need to tell me, I would welcome your truth, too.

Love,

Vanessa

I continued to write to them on holidays, Grace's birthday, and every now and then to let them know I was thinking of them. I was embarrassed that it had ended so badly, so ungraciously. Still, nothing. They were mad.

I wanted to make sure Grace had a clear path to them if she ever needed them. I also wanted to tell them I was sorry for pushing my Middle-Class White Girl Solutions to Homeless Problems on them. What they needed would have to come from deep inside them. It would take a systemic shift to make it more worthwhile to work, to facilitate job searching, to help the chicken-egg cycle of being unemployable, and, when you are employable, to make enough money so it beats out public assistance. Which they refused because they don't want to be part of the system.

One bright April morning I was outside talking to the neighbor, and I glanced down the block and noticed a young girl with long brown hair down to the small of her back. She had legs that went up forever, and I stopped; I thought for a moment it might be Bridgett. It wasn't. But the next thought was: This lanky fawn creature is Grace Future.

And then the girl bounced up and down because she saw her friend, and she waved and yelled. She seemed so happy in those few seconds. I realized definitively that it was not Bridgett. The Bridgett I know, even at her most mirthful, is quiet and measured. It's hard to imagine her express happiness with any flamboyance. I often wonder who she would be without Bill. I'd love to see her alone for a few days and find out if she unfurls.

And in that moment I prayed with everything I had for Grace to be the other girl. The happy one. The one who bounces when she sees her friend. And so far she is—most of the time, her gait isn't so much a walk as it is a jumping dance, whether she's entering the schoolyard loaded down, with her rainbow backpack dwarfing her skinny frame, or skipping through the aisle at Trader Joe's, holding up a new exotic snack for my approval (cue big brown doe eyes and the sound "mmmmm?"). She is a happy child, from everything I can tell.

My parents taught me, perhaps inadvertently, the art of nonattachment. People will come and go. They will die or turn on you or ask for more than you're willing to give. You should never really need anyone as an adult, though I'm beyond grateful that I get to be the person Grace needs while she's still little.

I hope to pass the best of what my parents gave me to her. But the greatest things I can give her are the tools to know and love her very own being. Because all you get in this lifetime is yourself, and everyone else is a gift given for an uncertain period of time.

PART IV

Rock Needs River

Sixteen

Following Signs

I'd decided shortly after Bill and Bridgett had lived with us that I wanted to write about us all, partly to document everything for Grace, to help explain her life. But also, there is so much untold about the relationship between adoptive and birth parents out in the world, and even less about the birth-parent experience. It became clear I needed to include Bridgett's and Bill's voices. They ignored my repeated attempts at connection. Finally, via a Facebook message, I asked them one last time if they would participate and tell their story—or help tell our story. They replied instantly.

"Sure, we're pretty open and easygoing about this stuff," Bill wrote.

I was shocked they said yes after so much silence—nearly two years' worth.

And that was how I found myself bumping along on a plane from LAX to San Antonio, the turbulence freaking me out and reminding me of my fragile mortality. As I hurtled toward the people who'd given me my resplendent child four and a half years before, I replayed a scene from the night before.

Me: "Is there anything you want to talk about before I go on my trip to see Bill and Bridgett?"

Grace: "I want to tell you something you tell me. I love you."

Then I started bawling, and Grace started fake crying with cartoonish sobs and shaking shoulders, making fun of me.

I love that little stinker.

I got off the plane in San Antonio, rattled, like I couldn't quite find my footing. In my twenties and thirties I'd traveled around the world in places that didn't speak English, with no more than a backpack, a ratty translation guide, and a few bucks in my pocket, and had done fine. But for this trip, I'd been compelled to share a detailed itinerary with my close friends, including the cryptic directions to Bill and Bridgett's home, for reasons I can't quite explain. I'd overpacked technology and weather items—extra cell-phone chargers, a recorder, a mic, lots of cords, boots, hats, rain gear. Just in case something went wrong. Bill and Bridgett were strangers once more, in a way. It had been nearly two years since they'd talked to me. I didn't want to lose them again.

As an alternative to their Los Angeles homelessness, Bill and Bridgett had moved to the Hill Country in Texas, an expanse that includes twenty-five counties, bridging Austin and north San Antonio. Bill had roots here, though I'd never seen two people more unhooked from their families. They'd moved into his grandmother's home, which had dubious ownership—it had been gifted to him, he said, then something about a deed and a relative and greed and now it was nobody's.

They had certainly been friendly enough and happy to tell their story, and had provided me with directions to their home, with no address, reachable only via rutted dirt roads and a short hop through some trees. They'd even invited Grace to come. I'd declined for her, though, for the same reason I stay elsewhere when visiting my mother. Intensity requires a proportionate amount of space. And if Grace had come, no work would have gotten done, and their truth wouldn't have come out as it did.

I'd wanted to buffer my trip by spending the first night with my friend Amy, who lives in San Antonio, but her house was filled with the flu. Which seemed quite fitting, that I'd do this alone. This was a solo journey. No friend or relative could do this for me or with me.

In my crappy little rental car, I set out from the airport, north on Interstate 10. My first impression: Texas is rambling and rocky under a surreally cerulean sky mapped out with fluffy white-silver clouds. It is bottles of blue and orange soda pop on ice. It is boots and drawls and salsa and peanut brittle. It is sawdust around a jukebox packed with Merle Haggard and Patsy Cline and Johnny Cash. It is the airplane hangar that became Leon Springs Dance Hall. It feels so, so American.

On Amy's recommendation I went to Rudy's Country Store and Bar-B-Q for lunch. I pondered the most impressive piece of turkey I'd ever tasted—brightly juicy and the right side of too salty—flanked by creamy sweet corn. As I lustfully eyed the peach cobbler I'd prudently planned to save for later, a family sat down behind me at the long outdoor table.

My grandpa Pat's brother Jimmy, Dad's uncle, was institutionalized in Warm Springs, Montana. Not that he'd done anything wrong. He just had a hard time getting a lock on the universe. He'd look at the stars piercing the black canopy of night and ponder their infinity, and while most of us regulate our thoughts when they reach their capacity to comprehend it all, he couldn't. His own mind would just spin endlessly. I understand this completely. I might have a little of what Jimmy had. Maybe that's why I'm on the constant lookout for signs about everything to assure myself I'm in the proper time-space coordinates in my life. Hummingbirds are check-ins from my dad—I put up a feeder on my porch so I can see them all the time and have a tattoo on my right bicep of a hummingbird feeding from a fuchsia flower, like my dad used to have at his home. I want to believe that crazy coincidences are some kind of high five from the universe. When the exact right song comes on the radio, or the lyric reflects something I've just said or thought, it means something. And on this day a conversation among complete strangers let me know I was on the right track, that I was supposed to be in the middle of Texas by myself at this moment.

"Want to sit with Grandma, Grace?" asked a female voice from the other table to a tiny girl, probably around two years old. "The first time you ate here, you were still inside Mommy."

The "Grandma, Grace" remark was my sign. I'd named my child after my grandmother Grace. It was my first cosmic clue that this trip was worth it all, that I was in the exact right place at the exact right time. It would have been nice to have someone with me who could share the haunting moment that referenced a child named Grace and being inside a mommy. I scribbled it all down in the crisp new journal I'd brought to document exactly these kinds of things. I didn't want to forget. And it became clear that yes, I needed to do this alone, or I'd miss the signs.

I continued on to Bandera, about an hour away, and tucked myself into the log cabin I'd rented at a guest ranch for the next several days. They'd doubled down on the Paul Bunyan–chic decor: timber bed frame and bunk beds, a rustic wooden table where I'd set up my computer and technical gear for recording interviews, and even wooden blinds.

I lay awake that first night willing time to go slowly until the chirping cicadas roared me to sleep.

The drive the next day took me along scrubby fields toward the swelling Medina River carved into a granite shore. It had been so long since I'd been near water like this. I marveled at the riparian system: All these slate-grey rocks need the river for their form and placement. A river needs rocks to give it a path, to slow it down and speed it up. Rocks and rivers are intrinsic opposites, yet they are critical components of each other, together and separately.

I pulled over and took pictures, my clunky leather Frye boots finding their footing along the smooth river rocks. Rain was imminent, confirmed by the silvery sky, and I envisioned myself stranded in my cheapo economy rental car and mentally prioritized which items I would protect (my computer, my recorder for Bill's and Bridgett's interviews) and which I would let be carried away by the water (yogurt, magazines, coffee).

The directions to Bridgett and Bill's home were something out of a paperback spy novel—no numbers, just "there's a roundabout at the end of the road, go left" kind of thing, which was just as well because the place was so remote there wasn't even a name for the town, and certainly no address. Or maybe at one point there had been an address, but the gravel road in front of the house was so heavily rutted and pitted that there was no way to access it. And anyway, I was too far from any kind of civilization for Siri on my phone to give any directions. She didn't care enough about people trying to survive way out here.

It had been a fruitless exercise to try and figure out exactly where I'd find them on any digital mapping system. I'd checked the directions dozens of times to make sure I wasn't missing anything. But what did I know? This was their turf, not mine. Surrender became the obvious—and only—choice.

On the last leg of the journey, where the directions became even more vague, I crept along the road, which turned from pavement to gravel to moonscape. I passed a modest manufactured home here and there—some with impeccable little yards; some with rusty mattress skeletons, parts of cars, old refrigerators, and furniture piled high, too bulky and expensive to haul to the dump. It seemed like the kind of place you'd land if you ran out of options everywhere else, or wanted to be at the end of the world, or were just born here and couldn't figure out how to leave.

I saw two lanky, long-haired figures walking toward me, their sneakers sure footed along the rutted road, gingerly pushing away gnarled juniper brush. Bill and Bridgett had come to guide me the rest of the way to their home. They looked exactly the same as every other time I'd seen them. They've got a pretty solid visual brand.

I pulled over. I breathed in nervousness that it was all happening now and breathed out relief that I'd found them and was one small step closer to connecting with them. After quick hugs, we all got in the car and drove another hundred feet or so. "You can pull over here," Bill said.

"Here?"

There was nothing. Just more scrubby trees and rocky road.

We got out. For whatever reason, though we'd not passed a soul, I felt like I needed to lock the car. Bill and Bridgett headed toward a short path through the pines, which led to a small house. It looked like it was manufactured perhaps in the 1960s or '70s. A porch of weathered two-by-fours sloped downward to create a sort of accidental ramp, as the supports underneath on one end had disintegrated. Siding that had probably once been painted a cheery yellow had taken on a rusty pall. A thick chain with a padlock hung from the metal door; the business end of a Pepsi soda fountain, awaiting exactly what, I wasn't sure. A motorbike, which needed more grease and parts and work than was worth it, leaned against the outside wall. Small plastic grocery bags containing trash were neatly tied to a gate to keep them out of the paws of critters.

I held my breath as Bill and Bridgett opened the door and led me inside.

I'm not sure what I expected but it wasn't this. I'd seen enough Detroit ruin porn—images of modern, haunting Pompeii-style decay that happened when residents fled the city seemingly midactivity, such as once-majestic theaters with tattered velvet seats and frescoed plaster peeling in great sheets from the ceiling, a piano buckling under the entropy of it all, or abandoned schoolrooms with books still open on the desks, buried under a thick layer of undisturbed dust—and imagined something like that. Maybe a musty old bedspread on a tired, droopy mattress, with granny wallpaper and a rotting floor. This? It was a home. A normal home that had been cleaned until it gleamed. Normal, except for no water and electricity, which would require a couple thousand dollars to restore. But a friendly neighbor supplied an extension cord so Bill and Bridgett could practice guitar, run a toaster oven, keep a light or two on, and watch movies on VHS. What the place lacked in curb appeal it made up for in impeccability. The door opened to a narrow wood-paneled living room, which contained a vintage '80s stereo and large, boxy TV, a black leather couch, a shiny coffee table. A glass-front cabinet held knickknacks and trophies, even a metallic globe.

If you'd been welcomed into this home thirty years ago, you'd have just assumed the people here lived more or less normal lives . . . save for the real coffin turned into a stand-alone cupboard outfitted with shelves, which housed Halloween-themed decorations—a skull, candles, dolls, and beer.

The primly made bed took up the entire bedroom. A third room was set up with Bridgett and Bill's guitars, drum kit, and amps against the backdrop of a wall-sized Texas flag. The bathroom was like any bathroom—sink, tub, toilet, and cupboard brimming with health and beauty items—except it had no running water.

A timeless, hermetically sealed vault.

I sat on the couch. Bridgett offered me the biggest coffee cake I'd ever seen, something you'd serve at a church function, perhaps. And some tea that tasted like fruit. She handed me some Hello Kitty stickers for Grace and a small bag of cranberry snacks, what you'd get on an airplane.

Ynnub the bunny scrambled around the floor, let out of her cage. She had somehow survived all their moves, all the Cheetos and tacos and people food and their extreme housing situations. I was relieved to see her still alive. I'd been afraid to ask about her.

I'd brought a book of photos of Grace from the past year. I'd been careful to include only pictures of her without me or her dad or other friends. I felt like I was selling a lifestyle spread that would be examined if not overtly, then on a subconscious level. See, she has fun! She plays dress up! She loves nature!

It felt like broaching new territory, after all this time without contact. How much was too much? Would these pictures just cause pain? Would it seem, in some way, like I was flaunting my motherhood?

"Would you like to see the pictures?" I asked. Bill politely said OK; Bridgett eagerly accepted, drinking in each image—Grace angel faced in a green princess dress the day before her fourth birthday, puddle hopping on the beach at sunset, in the bath surrounded by mounds of bubbles. I asked Bridgett if she wanted to keep the book. Yes, she did. Which made me happy. And then she took out her old Blackberry, which was out of minutes, and showed me pictures of Grace in the moments after she was born. Pictures I had never seen. I gave her twenty dollars to buy more minutes and send them to me. Still waiting to get them.

We talked a little about post–Los Angeles life. They desperately wanted to go back to do their music and get back into a more artistic routine in an urban setting. And they just loved LA and felt that was where their future was. They had gear packed and ready to go in the event of a last-minute ride-share offer. But then there was the question of what they'd do once they got back to Southern California. They'd traded the harshness of being homeless in a dangerous place for living in a different kind of survival mode—trudging a mile or more to the laundromat to fill up gallon jugs of water. Getting food from the church. Catching a ride from a friend or neighbor to the Lakehills Area Library, where they did all their computer stuff—Facebook, emails, scouring Craigslist for a ride out.

They had barely any money and spent barely any. They didn't want to get locked into any kind of welfare system in Texas, not when they felt they should spring back to LA at any second. They weren't anticonsumers; they were just nearly invisible on any sort of economic measure.

At home, they practiced their music or watched VHS tapes they could buy for a quarter at the library. They didn't check out books or movies because they never knew when they could come back to return them.

Bill showed me how he'd been filling his downtime. First, he pulled out a ream of white paper. Each side of each page was filled with tiny handwriting in black pen: his autobiography, *Hey Billy . . . Que Paso?*

The other thing he showed me was a game he and Bridgett invented. It's called Hands of Destiny, and it involves a multisided die, some cards with anime-style characters Bridgett drew, a musical timer that plays their original songs, and lots of swapping and stealing from other players. Bill had even written down ideas for the box design:

"Become
Smarter! Faster! Happier!
Your New BFF
Futuristic Display
Control the Universe
Collect and Trade
Challenge Your Friends
Be Better at Everything!!!"

He said he designed the game so that you can't cheat and even a little kid can beat someone older. They explained how it worked and all the twists that could happen until my head started to swim. It was like a mash-up of every card and board and strategy game invented, with wild cards strewn throughout. "The only thing you have to do to win this game is pay attention," he said. Because your fate could turn in an instant.

He explained what the game would look like, if it ever got made. A slick, colorful box and some plastic device that would play their music. A thick deck of cards, and then maybe Bridgett could have a comic book spin-off. As much as I've wanted them to win since the time I met them, perhaps this, above all, made me want them to win. To get something—anything—for what they'd created in the world.

And then we all got in the car. Our first stop was Medina Lake. Rain had been scarce, and now the lake was a vast crater with a puddle at the bottom. The joints that used to hop with music and beer and barbecue were now boarded up. Bill had me pull over at what used to be the Roadhouse honky-tonk. Thick dust coated what furniture remained inside—stacked chairs, overturned tables. The paint had peeled so badly you'd need to sandblast the whole thing and start over to make it right. He peered inside, past the "For Sale" sign, to the room that saw its last customers years ago. He used to work here, busing dishes and playing guitar. Nobody wanted it now. When the lake goes away, so do the people.

We headed to the Lakehills Area Library, where I interviewed Bill and Bridgett about their lives. They liked the library. They could check email here, and this was a chance for them to get a ride there without having to thumb it. I wanted to know the beginning of their stories, what happened after Grace was born, and how it all led to now.

At the end of day two of our interview sessions, we were talked out. We drove to the San Antonio suburbs so they could restock. I slipped them some cash, and Bill bought a twenty-dollar pair of new sneakers at Ross and threw his worn, tattered ones in the trash. At Walmart, they filled a cart with underwear for Bridgett, gloves for both of them, rabbit food, a water-filter pitcher, malt liquor, chili they loved that cost fifty cents a can. Bill considered two heads of iceberg lettuce, which to me seemed identical. They cost the same. He weighed them and chose the one that was an ounce heavier. At checkout, Bridgett wanted a Monster Energy drink. She was torn—should they spend the $2.50; was that too expensive? Bill made her get it.

We headed to Bill Miller Bar-B-Q, one of Bill's favorite barbecue joints. They ate like people who didn't ever get to eat out—ravenous. Thorough. There was not a crumb left over. Bill scrutinized the receipt on the tray and saw the number 405. His birthday in reverse. Where I look for meaning in signs from the universe, he finds them in number combinations. He said when he met Peter and me, he ran a set of numbers on a computer program he'd designed and surmised we wouldn't be married long. I dropped them at home and went back to my little cabin, where I numbed my mind by watching a mindless show with painfully unfunny jokes.

The next morning I kicked around the small town of Bandera, the self-proclaimed cowboy capital of the world. It's a main street with the requisite saloons, antique stores, tourist traps, and a high-end coffee haven. I ate breakfast at a sprawling diner, the walls lined with Western movie stars—heavy on the John Wayne paraphernalia; I downed a scrambled egg, a cheese and sausage burrito, and a cup of tea. The bill came to less than four dollars.

I made my way down a narrow staircase to one of the most famous joints around, the Silver Dollar, a honky-tonk with sawdust floors. There was a jukebox, of course, and a pool table and an old-timey scale on which you could weigh yourself for five cents. A stage in the corner for live music. The long tables that spanned the room were mostly empty, except for one, with three grizzled cowboys, who watched *The Price Is Right*, their gazes glued to the screen above the bar. I took some pictures and said "Thank you," and nobody moved a muscle or uttered a word as I took my city-girl ass out of there.

Next, I wandered into an arty little store, picked out a couple souvenirs for people back home, and started talking to the woman behind the counter. Friendly, in her early fifties. She asked, like everyone I encountered, what I was doing in town. Usually I said, "Just visiting friends." But this time, for whatever reason, I answered, "Talking to people for a book." She pressed me and wanted to know what the book was about. "It's my daughter's birth parents. I wanted to know more about their story and their adoption experience."

When I mention adoption to anyone I don't really know, I usually get a smile and nod and some kind of affirmation—"Oh! My sister adopted two boys!" or "I'm adopted" or some variation on how lucky my child is ("I'm the lucky one," I always answer. I just don't go deep on that with strangers). But this woman suddenly became very still and quiet. I wondered if I'd said something wrong.

And then this: "Thirty years ago, I gave up my son for adoption," she said. She told me the story about how young she was. How hard she was working as a waitress and how she could barely feed herself. How she absolutely wasn't ready to be a mother. During her pregnancy, she worked a conference-catering gig at a hotel, and the speaker was Kathleen Silber, the open-adoption advocate. Riveted, she listened to her speak about something nobody had ever really considered, this new concept of open adoption. She approached Silber afterward, who connected her with all the resources she'd need. "We had the first open adoption in Texas," she said.

She'd stayed connected to her son. They had a good relationship, and she had just become a new grandmother. But it wasn't all happy. She remembers lying there in the hospital after handing over the baby to his new parents. Nobody in her life supported her choice—not her parents and not her friends. "I woke up, and they'd all abandoned me," she said.

Even today, she tells hardly anyone her story. She doesn't want to risk the judgment that inevitably follows.

She handed me her card, which was destroyed hours later when I accidentally spilled tea all over it. I'd like to think I'll see her again someday, though.

By noon, it was time to go see Bill and Bridgett, our last day together. We'd planned for me to make a video of them playing music that I could bring home to show Grace or that maybe they could load up to YouTube. But instead, as soon as I walked in the door, they sat me down on the couch. There was a compact video recorder set up on a tripod, and they said they wanted to tell me their full, unadulterated version of what happened before, during, and after Grace's birth. Bill did all the talking.

Their experience, in the end, was ugly, humiliating. Scary. They felt, basically, like baby machines after their adoption experience—they were chattel to social workers, with the baby as the valuable commodity; they were marginalized in the hospital when they tried to assert their rights to hand over their child; they were garbage when they were abandoned by the agency in the face of medical bills that went unpaid. Bill insisted on my asking him questions, talk-show style, which he answered. It was as if this particular strain of rage, which he'd held for more than four years, had finally busted through a dam.

After a couple hours of fielding hard, harsh truth—and it did finally feel like truth—I needed to decompress in the most desperate way. I took a walk along the slow-rolling river, which cuts through Bandera. I felt so far away from home. I pondered the great fortune that Grace had gotten the best of Bill and Bridgett to become this perfect, magical little being. I met some feral kittens parked out on a picnic bench, and stopped to sit in an old, crazy-growing tree whose trunk curved around my body like a cradle. Out in the Hill Country, my heart beat notice-ably slower. I missed Grace fiercely and couldn't wait to wrap myself around her, and remind myself that she is mine and that I am hers.

And then I needed to get as far away as possible. I needed a beauty I couldn't access from my little log-cabin room, and my plane home wasn't for another day. I'd been nervous about all the rain and the flash-flood warnings on the radio inserted in between country songs. Still, through sheets of water, under cracks of lightning, I drove north as far and as fast as I could, out of town. I passed signs warning of swollen creeks. Cattle blissfully unaware of the rain and their ranchers' endgame. Trees with sprawling, leafy canopies; pinpoint towns. The road narrowed and twisted so severely at points that I had to open the window and gulp in air so I wouldn't get sick. And at sunset, I ended in Kerrville, twenty-five miles away, an arty, small city. The clouds had pulled apart and become fluffy peach-and-pink confections, the sun slicing through. A rainbow stretched bright and full across the sky. It was a sign of something. Not sure what, but something. I window-shopped, bought seven sparkly rings at a deep discount in an antique store, ate dinner, and drove back to my Paul Bunyan room.

The next morning I packed my gear and headed for San Antonio. My one friend there was still sick with the flu, but on the phone she guided me through town toward lunch at a place called the Lincoln, a former school with a pink-painted exterior and the inside tricked out as a bistro. I hung up and sat in the parking lot, where I sobbed. The heavy weight of Bill and Bridgett's suffering had crushed me, forcing out tears and anguish. There was rage mixed in there as well—rage that all I'd tried to do to help them didn't matter. And that they didn't help themselves. And also a smattering of self-pity. I was so, so, so tired of taking care of everyone.

After a good forty-five minutes, I was out of tears. An exceptionally well-timed call from a best girlfriend set me as normal as I could get. I went in, ate, and had more time to kill before my plane. I drove around San Antonio, wearing my homesickness like a heavy robe. I found myself at the Mission Concepción, a 1716 structure built by the Spanish, with the intent to teach Native Americans about "civilized" ways. The sanctuary was empty, dimly lit to an amber glow. It was early November, just after Día de los Muertos, and an altar in the front of the church overflowed with photos and mementos of loved ones gone amid marigolds, corn husks, and small plastic skeletons and skulls. A vintage 1980s school picture of a teenage girl, who would have probably been my age now; a couple wearing leis under a banner that read, "Welcome to Hawaii!"; a pair of baby shoes. So much missing.

Alone, I sat on a hard wooden chair in front of the hero image, a portrait of Mary. Tears slipped down my face. I wanted to ask her something while I had the chance. I couldn't think of anything interesting, so I just said, quietly, "I want you to know that I tried. I tried so hard."

And a moment later, a docent came in leading two people. He was unnecessarily loud in the silent space, shouting away my private audience with Mary. I left.

I got on a plane and came home.

Seventeen

One Thing I Didn't Mention

In the spring of 2017, Bill and Bridgett found someone from Craigslist to give them a ride from Texas to LA. They described him as an arrogant jerk—he didn't want to stop at Target or anywhere on the way so they could get supplies and food for the trip. He was so hell-bent on getting to Mexico that he wouldn't even leave them in LA or San Diego—they had to make their way back from the border, they said. The VA put them up in a Motel 6 for a while and then said a place would be ready for them within two months. Finally, Bill thought, they'd found someone who actually respected veterans and could help.

But their hotel funds ran out before they could get housed, and they tried camping out in downtown San Diego. "Those homeless people are really scary—much worse than in LA. Mean. We didn't feel safe," Bill said.

They contacted me and asked me to bring another pair of glasses for Bill—theirs were stolen, along with their IDs, they said. They decided San Diego wasn't that great after all, and returned to LA and waited.

We met at the park downtown, where we used to meet when Grace was little. Grace, now six, asked Bridgett to play with her on a bee with a huge spring under it that made it pitch back and forth when they rocked it. Bill helped her tap out "Mary Had a Little Lamb" on a metal music toy. He remarked on her excellent timing and rhythm.

Next we stopped for burritos and sat at a long, high wooden table. Grace told them about learning piano—her teacher thinks she is a prodigy and is constantly surprised at how adept she is at learning and remembering songs.

The conversation shifted to something grown-up, the logistics of their move. And Grace was trying to get my attention, climbing up on me, playing with my hair, refusing to be ignored.

"She reminds me of my daughter," Bill said.

The air froze for a minute, and I asked for clarification. "You have another child?"

"Oh? I never told you? Had."

He told me the story, after all these years of never mentioning it.

It was 1999, and he was playing out, got drunk after a show, and went home with a girl, whom he described as "a mess, had a whole bunch of other kids and was also married, but it was complicated." He was pretty sure the baby was his, though.

They named the child Wendy Diane, and she lived with the mother. She was just a little thing when Child Protective Services swooped in—there was nothing to eat in the house, and the mother was AWOL. So Bill got custody of her, and the judge told the mother to stop having kids, Bill said.

For three years, Bill was Wendy Diane's full-time dad. He taught her music. They had fun together. But Wendy Diane's grandfather was a millionaire doctor and promised Bill that if he didn't hand over custody, they'd be tied up in court forever. Bill said he didn't want that for Wendy Diane, so he relinquished all rights.

He missed that little girl. Terribly. He wasn't even allowed to visit her, he said.

Three years later, in 2006, he was in a Hill Country bar, and a friend came up to him and said, "I'm so sorry about what happened with your daughter."

And Bill replied that it had been a long time since he'd seen her and he was getting used to it.

"No," the friend said, "she died."

Apparently her older half sister had just learned to drive. She was fifteen and took Wendy Diane driving out on that winding road through Lakehills and crashed the car. Neither of them made it.

Bill wrote a song with his band, the Paramount Blues Review, called "Allways"—the two *l*'s are on purpose. In it, he sings about his undying love for his little girl.

I know with great certainty that if anything ever happened to Grace, I would not survive it. I can't imagine that kind of pain.

"The way I see it, God gives us people and takes them away. And if that didn't happen like it did, I probably wouldn't have come here, met Bridgett, and there would be no Grace," he said there in the Chipotle, finishing up his burrito. It is remarkable to me how Bill can make sense of crazy situations.

I felt flattened and held back tears. All I could think to say was, "I'm so sorry, I'm so sorry."

I wondered if this could be true. And if it was, why didn't he tell me before?

And then, as much as my heart was shattered for this small, unfortunate girl who had such a short, little life, the pieces fused together stronger for Bill. This loss explained so much to me. I understood, in that moment, his reluctance to become a parent again. The deep, unthinkable wound he carries everywhere. Why he loves Grace from so far away, even in the moments they're together.

I went home and looked up his song on a site called SoundClick. And there it was. "Allways." The photo next to the song was of a little girl with shiny, curly platinum hair, in a princess dress, holding a small

blue Flying V electric guitar in front of a microphone. Exactly something Grace would do.

I will forever be haunted by the thought of Grace's missing sister.
Even if it's not true.

Eighteen

WE ARE ALL ORPHANS

I'm generally very "rah, rah! Adoption is amazing!" around Grace when the subject comes up. I never, ever wanted her to have an untrue version of her origin story. I never wanted her to have fantasies about her birth parents. I wanted her to always understand how grateful I am that we found each other and how astounding and amazing it was that Bill and Bridgett knew to pick the absolute perfect mommy and daddy for her. I made her a book for her second birthday, called *The Book of Grace*, and it opens with a tiny baby spirit looking for a family. There's a page with pictures of Bill and Bridgett playing music, looking happy. Another page with pictures of me and her dad taken for our adoptive-parent profile shortly before we became parents. We are relaxed, a little windswept, clean, and American, like people in a vitamin ad.

The next pages in the book show the day Grace was born. There's the wailing new baby picture; one of Bridgett in a hospital gown, smiling down beatifically upon her; one of Bridgett leaning into Bill, the baby off on the side, sleeping. Every combination of every parent holding her. And then the book chronicles her first visits from friends, family, neighbors, and her grandparents. There are pictures of her striking a ridiculous fashion-pout pose, wearing a woolly lamb's costume, eating some of the pile of snow she's lying in, "playing" guitar. There are some at the relinquishment procedure two weeks after she was born, one of the paper-signing milestones at the agency that we had to do with Bill and Bridgett, in which Grace is wrapped in my orange wool sweater in Bridgett's arms. There are some joyous ones of the legalization ceremony at a courthouse a month shy of her first birthday—immediate family and friends came to document the occasion, kind of like a courthouse wedding. I made the book because I wanted her to know how celebrated she was, how much she means to all of us. That the way she came to be our child was perfect, the way it was supposed to be.

There is hardly ever a time when I don't look at her and see them. Sometimes it is a physical reminder: Grace's big brown eyes and her shoulders, those are all Bill; the way Grace says "yeah" or "sure" in a quiet, breathy way is exactly Bridgett. Bridgett also gifted her with lean, strong legs; her bow-like, pink little mouth; her deep, deep sweetness and intense desire to be helpful. Grace has Bill's capacity for math and seeing patterns everywhere. Grace and Bridgett are both organizers: they make every place better than they found it. I see a propensity toward anxiety and perfectionism, and I suspect that may be passed from Bridgett. As of this writing, with kindergarten and first grade conquered, Grace has never been absent or late to school. Sometimes, she'll ask, mounting panic in her voice, "Will I be late?"

"No, baby, we won't. We'll be on time. But you know what? It's no big deal if we are late," I say.

"Yes, it is!" she says, in a high whine. I tell her to look at the clock and see that no, we won't be late. And she is assured and goes into the schoolyard, only when she can find a friend who will walk with her from the gate to their class group.

But Grace also loves to be on stage and will put on a show for anyone who will watch. She'll flop herself around the living room in elaborate choreography—think Twyla Tharp participating in some ancient

Greek field events—and tell people proudly that she's "self-taught." She's the first to raise her hand when a magician needs a volunteer. Her timing was perfect when she had the one line in a school musical about losing teeth. The cue was: "Why do dentists love potatoes?" and she belted out, in the way little kids on stage do, quickly but loud so you can hear in the back, "Oh! I know this one: because they're so *filling*!"

Her love of being on stage, that comes from all of us, me and Peter, Bridgett and Bill.

Adoption. What's not to love?

Some of it and none of it and all of it, if you ask Grace.

She rarely talks about her own adoption, or Bill and Bridgett, or adoption in general, and maybe that's because it's so normal for her. Like talking about air or trees. Once, we'd gone to a lovely dinner at the home of her preschool friend Freddy. The boy had a doll that switched from *Frozen*'s Elsa to Anna when you turned it upside down and flipped the skirt over, which became the new high bar for toys, as far as Grace was concerned. They also dressed up in costumes, and messed up his impeccable bedroom, and ran around like little maniacs. Normal kid stuff. When we came back home, as I was helping her change into pajamas, I said, "Hey, did you know that Freddy is adopted, too?"

She looked at me as if I'd said something ridiculous. Like that bubble gum comes out of rabbit butts.

"Some people aren't adopted?" she asked.

We'd made adoption such an everyday thing it was part of her daily world order.

Another night, after a brief reading of Jamie Lee Curtis's *Tell Me Again About the Night I Was Born*, a book about a family coming together through adoption, she tossed the book aside and said, "We'll give this to the library." She also had no time for *And Tango Makes Three*, a veiled adoption parable about a pair of penguins who take on a third; she quickly jettisoned that book, too.

One Mother's Day, over oatmeal and fried eggs for breakfast, I was talking about how important it was for us to think about Bridgett and Bill and honor them. She replied, in all seriousness, "Mom, but Mother's Day is for families." I tried to explain that Bridgett and Bill were also family, and she thought about that. Of course I want her to tap them if she ever needs them—or for them to see her if they ever want to—but most of me is relieved that I am number-one mama, as far as she's concerned. Since she's been able to write, I've gotten a nearly daily love letter with pictures of us together, flanked by bunnies and flowers and stars, all some variation of "I love Mom."

I think about her inevitable abandonment wound that stems from a deep, deep place inside her. Most of the time, you'd never know—she seems fine being around Bridgett and Bill.

But once, a month or so after Bridgett and Bill moved out, we were making dinner and Grace had taken her customary seat on the counter, next to the sink, to "help." I asked her, offhand, if she ever thought about them.

"I like Bridgett, but I don't like Bill," she said.

She was a few months away from turning three, and up until then, she'd never expressed that she didn't like someone.

"Why don't you like Bill?"

She thought a moment. "He lied." The hair on my arms stood up. How did she even know what a lie was?

"What did he lie about?"

"He lied about me."

"What makes you think that?" I stammered.

She didn't answer any more questions and went back to playing with a measuring cup.

There are those creepy stories about toddlers who start speaking Russian for no reason and talk about how they died at sea; a would-be twin who speaks of a sibling who died in the womb; five-year-olds who "remember" something about the neighborhood from before they were born, from the last time they were alive. This felt like that. Like something she couldn't possibly know or remember in her short, little life so far. In her world she'd never even experienced a lie. I'm convinced she'd had a deep, spiritual in utero understanding that Bill and Bridgett had kept the pregnancy and Grace's existence a secret from their families. Could it be some deep kind of baby rage coming out from inside? Or a disappointment expressed in a concept I hadn't even realized she fully comprehended? I don't know why Bridgett got a pass on this and Bill didn't—unless there was deeper, hidden information that only she had access to. This child. This child knew something. Not from me. I'd been very careful to talk about Bill and Bridgett only in the most positive light.

Grace knew her adoption story in and out. She'd gone through periods where she wanted nothing to do with *The Book of Grace*, and times when she wanted to look at it over and over again, even to the point of being proud enough to bring it to show-and-tell at school.

~

The Book of Grace is tiny, a few pages, a few pictures. But it is part of a larger whole. The little, personal thing is universal. Nearly every epic story is about adoption. A king learns by prophecy that his infant son will someday kill him. In an effort to thwart fate, the king pierces the babe's ankles and hands him to a servant, who leaves him on a hillside to die from exposure. But all is not lost! A shepherd and his wife find the child and raise him as their own. Many years later, as an adult, the child meets his father in a crossroads, kills him in a fit of road rage, and unknowingly marries the king's wife, his own biological mother, the queen. When he realizes what has happened, he blinds himself in a fit of anguished remorse, and doom settles upon the kingdom.

This is, of course, the story of Oedipus, one of mythology's more unfortunate adoptees. There are thousands of stories that evolve from and revolve around the theme of adoption—we've been enthralled with the question of origin and family since we started telling stories. The Bible and Greek and Roman mythology tell tale after tale of children being raised by other parents—sometimes human, sometimes not. (Think Romulus and Remus and the she-wolf who nursed them after they were thrown into the Tiber River.) Since the very first day of my freshman Mythology 101 class at NYU, I've been captivated with stories and how the Etruscans and Greeks set the stage for so much of the Western world we "enjoy" today, for better or worse. I was so enthralled that I became a classics major and am still friends with my Latin professor, Elizabeth Scharffenberger, one of the foremost classicists in the country. I asked her to further illuminate the adoption theme for me. She said that in the typical classical myth, a child is left to die and is then taken in by others until the true parentage or heritage is revealed to either fortunate or terrible consequences. The stories frequently center on identity, and often the origination of the adoption is a way to hide a child from a fate laid down by a prophecy, decreed by a god, or exercised by an evil regime, Elizabeth said. Yes, poor Oedipus. But the later story of Moses from the Bible has a happier ending: The Egyptian pharaoh's henchmen are out for the blood of infant Jewish boys. When Moses's mother realizes she can't keep him safe, she packs him in a basket and floats him down a river, where he is found and reared by the pharaoh's daughter, Bithiah. Moses eventually leads the Jews to safety.

Everyone loves a road trip. And indeed, nearly every epic story is about a journey that reflects, in some way, our own. A classic hero/heroine tale begins with a disturbance or abandonment. The child finds support from a completely different kind of family—another socioeconomic class, fairies, witches, or even animals. Let's remember Dorothy Gale in *The Wizard of Oz*: An orphan, she finds a home, albeit grey and dowdy, with her auntie Em and uncle Henry. Dorothy discovers a new family of sorts when she leaves Kansas and meets a Tin Man, Cowardly Lion, and Scarecrow. The hero or heroine is then forced to find a new tribe—sometimes it's by marrying a prince (Oh hi, Cinderella, Snow White, and Sleeping Beauty!); sometimes it's by discovering a kinship (Tarzan, raised by apes from infancy, found a human wife in Jane; orphan Harry Potter was unofficially adopted by the Weasley family of the wizarding world). Or consider the excruciating dynamics in two storylines from contemporary entertainment. In the PBS miniseries *Downton Abbey*, the brokenhearted, unmarried Edith bears a child, Marigold, and must hand her over to a Swiss family, then to a local farming family, the Drewes, so as not to further soil her family's already-shaky reputation. The snatch-back and jockeying-for-position scenes between Edith and Mrs. Drewe are nothing short of brutal, magnifying the pain of the birth mother, adoptive mother, and the child in the middle. NBC's *This Is Us* poses the powerful scenario of a black baby adopted as a newborn by a white family. The character of Randall undergoes a lifetime of anguish for not knowing his birth father. His feelings are further compounded when he learns his mother kept the identity of the birth father a secret, in part to protect him, in part to secure her own feelings of motherhood. In so many of these stories, there is always winning and losing. In young Dorothy's case, all seems lost when she can't return home, but once she does, she sees her family through a new lens of love and appreciation. She has changed, and that enables her to be, in her heart, home. But that is a happy fiction.

"Often when the adventure starts, it's somebody who thought they were in a secure family but discovered that they're not in a secure family situation," said Nancy Mellon, MA, who delightfully describes herself as "an elder in the global storytelling renaissance." An author, psychotherapist, and mentor, she uses storytelling as a tool for healing. She hammers home what all of us already know on some level: she says that nearly every story, from every time period, is about the journey the hero undergoes to find his or her new family or return to an original

one. The highly personal tale of self-discovery is also the most universal. Many of us carry core abandonment wounds for various reasons,
but for adoptees, that wound digs deeper. That shows up especially in
mythology. Mellon said that children have an ever-present feeling and
fear of abandonment, even if their mother is at home, in their physical
presence. These feelings evolve and mutate as we grow, much of the time
in a healthy way, but sometimes not. The seed is there, whether you're
legally adopted or in a tightly knit biological family. In fact, once you
recognize the prevalence of the original/new family theme in stories,
you can never unsee it. It's everywhere.

~

Even if she's not telling her story directly, I know Grace reckons with
her adoption by the way she plays. Starting when she was five, there
was the daily rendition of Puppy School, in which I adopt her as a dog,
and lo, we discover that she is a magic puppy! And that I am actually a
queen! And then we pretend to change things around the house with
lasers from our fingers. This game was originally called Orphanage and
involved me, a mom/queen, picking out a child, but I put the kibosh on
that, explaining that we shouldn't play about such a serious topic that's
real for a lot of kids. Now it has evolved into a kind of fancy boarding-
school scenario in which we are princess sisters (she gets to be Rose, and
I have the unfortunate name of Doze) and we enter a lot of cooking
competitions and take limousine rides and find out things from invisible air computers. She's not yet had a question about Bridgett and Bill,
except about why they're homeless, when we brought them supplies
after a fire wiped out their urban campsite—and she insisted on giving
them a twenty-dollar bill a friend had folded for her in a complicated
origami. It broke my heart—it's not her job to take care of them—but
I didn't want to quash her generosity. It was hard to find the words to
explain why they didn't have a normal apartment. I probably bungled

that one and talked about the importance of hard work and the choices we make in our lives.

She knows I'm her forever mama, and sometimes she seems wistful—when she was little she would make an instinctual, primal beeline for my breasts at the hope of feeding. I think we both were a little sad that never happened for us. And I will always remember a picture she drew when she was about three, of what looked like a mom and baby. "Is that me holding you?" I asked.

"No," she said. "It's me growing in your tummy."

It's my life goal to be the mother Grace wants and needs. I've been on a crusade to raise her to value kindness, generosity, and equality. I offer unconditional love to her and will drop everything when she asks for affection. I hope that at nighttime cuddles she never, ever stops asking for "one more minute," which she does, every single time.

She is also smart and brave and teaches me things every day. Once, when she was nearly four, she looked at a plaque I kept near my desk, a leftover relic from my working in an office.

She considered the black blotchy typewriter font on white metal and asked me, "What does it say?"

I read it to her: "What would you do if you could not fail?"

With that, she took it off the pin board. "We don't need this. We don't fail," she said, and marched it to the trash. I was stunned. God, please grant me the confidence of this sweet, fierce baby girl.

I've gone after those who have presented sexist microbullshit particles that eventually become waves: I called out the karate teacher who complimented the boys' strength and attitude but praised the girls for their smiles; I wrote to the library about a book that showed all the male superheroes flying, holding buildings, and saving people, but Wonder Woman's job in that book was to push a child on a swing; I tried to explain to the class parent who romanticized the sole five-year-old boy at a group playdate as a "ladies' man" just how shitty that was for the girls and the boys. Extreme and minute patriarchy doesn't serve anyone well.

I hope the hard work will pay off and that Grace and I will love each other dearly, madly, joyfully, and grow to become old ladies sitting on a porch, reminiscing about our lives together and feeling so happy and lucky we found each other in this big old world.

Nineteen

A Surprise Beginning

Around the time she turned five, Grace presented an alternate origin story. It was her story to own and tell. A story so powerful that it became a tattoo that takes up my left forearm, from wrist to elbow.

We were walking along the sidewalk in our neighborhood on a balmy afternoon, the sun shining low and hot in the sky.

Apropos of nothing obvious, Grace stopped me, suddenly.

"Mama, pretend that I'm a baby and you found me next to this tree."

"OK," I said, listening hard. As usual, she was going to be the writer and director of this story, and I was just an actor allowed an occasional improv.

She hid behind the tree, which was about as skinny as she was. I pretended to walk by and suddenly see her. She crouched shyly.

"Hi, little baby, are you scared?" I asked her, kneeling down. She nodded seriously, big brown eyes taking up half her face.

"You look like you're all alone, would you like to come home with me?"

"Yes," she said.

"What's your name?"

"Magnolia. I'm named that because this is a magnolia tree. I grew in a flower. A butterfly brought me nectar, and bees and squirrels brought me honey and juice."

"You grew very big."

"Yes," she said. "I'm too big for the flower now. The animals said they would find me a mommy. And you live so close to here. They said you'd be the best mommy."

"I'll take good care of you, and you can come home with me. I have a beautiful room for you. I'll be your mommy forever and ever. Would you like that?"

"Yes," she said, taking my hand and walking toward home. "Yes, I would."

AFTERWORD

Peter and I have eased into a good balance in our parenting; we have tried to be accommodating toward each other as schedules shift and change around Girl Scouts and birthday parties and holidays and my occasional work travel. His older daughters have blossomed into beautiful, supercool young adults, and they adore Grace; she's happy to have sisters and also an older brother, who comes with a lovely wife and a growing brood of boys her own age. Peter moved an hour away, back to his hometown near the beach by his parents. Grace sees him every other weekend and spends extra time with him on vacation. She likes it. She gets unlimited TV there and also Lunchables, which have never, ever entered our organic, free-range, hippie kale bean sprouts kitchen. (I've chosen my battles; this is not one of them.) She loves him, which is what I care about the most. He lives with a very nice lady, who also loves Grace and takes her to get manicures and decorates Christmas cookies with her. This makes me immensely relieved, that there's another grown-up on site. Just in case.

I worry about his health, still. And these days, the alcohol issue is a dance: I sometimes ask about the smell, which is there to varying degrees, and Peter insists he doesn't know where it comes from, or he denies there is any smell—so of course I Google that, and lo, there is a medical condition that does cause an alcohol smell in someone who hasn't been drinking. And then I say, in all earnestness, "Oh, then you probably have a terrible medical condition. I hope you get that looked at." Every. Single. Time. I suspect I will always be worried about his drinking and he will also flat-out deny any alcohol abuse, forever.

I'm more than 99 percent certain that Peter doesn't drive drunk with Grace in the car. But I keep a continuous ticker of a prayer going for her safety. It is always there. It never stops.

I don't know what to write about Bill and Bridgett. They remain furious about their adoption experience and how they were treated. They're still battling for the brutal life they've chosen—or that's been chosen for them—in downtown LA. They've come in and out of our lives several times; as of this writing, they're out, by their own volition, and in the middle of a text conversation, they became angry with me for reasons I don't quite understand but have tried to dissect many times over. I will forever hope that they can change their fate and fortune. I also hope they will be available for Grace should she ever need them. They know where to find us.

As for Grace, she continues to be the greatest love of my life. She is gifted on the piano, an impatient and quick learner. She is kind to our weird little schnoodle dog and runs around with a pack of sweet-faced girlfriends at school, hunting for fairies and building houses for them. She does crappy magic tricks that are unintentionally hilarious. Every night, we read a book in her bed or in mine, and I switch off the light and we snuggle until she's close to sleeping. As I get up, I say a prayer over her, sometimes silently, sometimes out loud. "Keep this child safe," I plead to whatever goddess or god is tuning in. And so far, they have.

ACKNOWLEDGMENTS

There are so many people to thank for getting this book into the world. It is staggering to me, and deeply humbling, to realize how not alone I was on this enterprise, even though it felt like that so many times.

I'll start with three editors, who helped me understand, at various stages of this work, that my story was compelling enough to tell widely: K. J. Dell'Antonia, who thought that a little episode of the birth parents moving in was novel enough for the *New York Times*. The very best acceptance letter I have ever received was from Jia Tolentino for a piece on my miscarriages. She wrote: "Holy shit, Vanessa, this is confoundingly beautiful . . . I would be honored to get to run it on *Jezebel*." And I've never seen an editor with as much compassion and as light a touch as Kaelyn Forde when she was at Refinery29 and ran a photo essay of my trip to see Bill and Bridgett in Texas. K. J., Jia, and Kaelyn, I'm forever yours, wherever you may roam.

Sorry about all those shitty first, second, and third drafts, to those who gave feedback on various versions of this manuscript. I'm deeply touched that you told me some hard truths about what just wasn't working, all in the effort to make it better. Joy Allen, Martina Clark, Meghan Cleary, Shannon Kelly Gould, Jack Hetherington, Jill Ivey, Amanda Koster, Alisha Krabinaus, Laurel Lathrop, Kaumudi Marathe, Sean McGrady, Amy Minton, Quynh Nguyen, Jessica Portner, Natalie Riggs, Lelah Simon, Matthew Specktor, Jeff Sweat, M. Rachel Thomas, and Pamela Toler, and anyone else I've inadvertently left out (and I'm so, so, so sorry if that's the case), I'm flabbergasted that you would be so generous with your time, talent, and input for this project in its various incarnations. Special shout-out to Jess Burnquist, who helped me whittle down my concept that "a rock and a river are totally opposite yet they need each other to be what they are" into the title I fell in love with.

Christina Hoffman, thank you for staying on the scene, from moment one when you sent over a picture of a baby gulping her first breaths, to the Batman birthday party, to the beach, and to whatever adventures come our way next. You are pure love and light. You are the bridge from New Grace to Now Grace.

So much of this book is about finding a tribe, and I don't know what I'd do without the people who have blessed me with their love and friendship through the years and played such a huge part in this story. Val and Will Aitcheson, Valentin Babakhanian, Sanjiv Bajaj, Sarika Chawla, Meghan Cleary, Joe Coultman, Sine DeSio, Pat DeVol Nadon, the Droisen/Waldron clan, Charlotte Eyerman, *la famille* Gayot, Melissa Jones, Amanda Koster, Liza Lewellen, Kathlyn Lewis, Kaumudi Marathe, Joanna Massey, Libby McInerney, Lisa McKenna, Mia Nakao, June Nery, Quynh Nguyen, Charles Papert, Alison Peacock, Linda Perkins, Jessica Portner, Natalie Riggs, Mara Schwartz, Martha Shade, Stephanie Simpson, Andrea Sluchan, Ellen and John Spiller, Robin Stevens, Nikki Taguilas, Ebonye Gussine Wilkins, and Annie Wharton, you give my life light and meaning.

To my motley bunch of darkly funny, angelically helpful women in a Facebook group who go by such an impolite collective noun I can't repeat it here, I can always count on your sassy, sublime support. And yes, cobbler will be fine, thank you.

It's true that there's strength in numbers, but there's also adoration. ASJA has the loveliest, most supportive people, especially here in the SoCal outpost: JoBeth McDaniel, David Groves, Stephen Siciliano, Beverly Gray, Linda Marsa, Barbara DeMarco-Barrett, and

Scott Stanley Smith, I'm humbled and inspired by your generosity of spirit and talent. My UPOD Academy cohort led by the godfather of all freelancers, David Hochman, felt like the grown-up version of *The Breakfast Club*, with all our soul sharing and crackling chemistry from being cooped up together for two days many years ago. Meghan Cleary, Nina Giovannitti, Melissa Goldstein, Carren Jao, Oliver Jones, Megy Karydes, Libby McInerney, Greg Nichols, Linda Perkins, Laura Shin, Erika Sieme, Niva Dorell Smith, and Robert Spuhler (and RIP, our dear Amy Dawes), you all taught me so much in so many different ways, and I love that we will always be Goats forever, together.

To the experts who showed the way: Melissa Dodson, Linda Brown, Ann Wrixon, Nancy Mellon, Kathleen Silber, and Liz Scharffenberger. Thank you for sharing your deep knowledge with me about how things work, in story and in life.

Jeff Sweat: It feels like we signed up for space camp at the same time, but you were dancing around on Mars while I was still figuring out how to put my helmet on. Thank you for leading me here and for being my best book buddy, karaoke partner (you're a bum, you're a punk), and a kind of brother to me.

Mr. Timpson, I will never, ever forget the moment of my delighted shock when you rushed into the coffee shop with flowers and Kleenex to celebrate the momentous news that this book had found its home. Thank you for shining your light on me. My, my, my. I love you.

Jaime Wolf, I appreciate your careful thought and sharp observation, and all the bits of knowledge wedged in that lovely brain of yours. Whew!

To Carmen Johnson, my editor, who kept finding sparkling diamonds under dust balls in order to make this book into its very best self: You're talented and kind and wise, and it's been so fun to work with you. You've given this manuscript its best possible life. Thank you for seeing the dream and making it happen.

Cheryl Pientka, my agent and now friend, believed in this book from the first moment she heard about it. She is the embodiment of infinite patience, knowledge, and insight. Cheryl is the kind of person you can call when you're feeling lonely and overwhelmed in Texas and need to talk to someone, anyone who will truly understand what a weird day you had. Cheryl, I'm sitting here typing this, crying with gratitude for all the work you put in to get *Rock Needs River* into the right hands. I know we met for a deeper reason than work. There just aren't enough ways to express how much you mean to me.

My family, the McGradys and the Robinsons, remind me who I am and who I can be. I am at home when I'm with you, wherever we are. Aunt Corky, Mom, Ilya, and Ian, thanks for lending your memories so that I could have a better picture of the complex truth of our lives. Lilliwaup forever. I love you all.

To Peter, thank you for helping to make me a mom and for loving our kid so well. I can't imagine being on this journey of parenthood with anyone but you.

Bridgett and Bill, you will forever have my love and gratitude for choosing us to become parents for Grace. I honor you every day for letting me love this child infinitely, and I thank you for all you bestowed upon her. She's truly lovely and got all the best parts of you both; I see that every day.

And finally, Grace, my magical fairy child, I'm beyond proud to be your mom. You make my life sparkle. I cherish our time together. I don't know how I got so lucky to become your mama. But I will never, ever take it for granted, and I'm thankful for you every second and every space in between those seconds. Every day I think it's impossible that I can love you more, yet every day I do.

ABOUT THE AUTHOR

Photo © 2016 Stephanie Simpson

Writer Vanessa McGrady spends time thinking about feminist parenting, high-vibrational food, and badass ways to do things better. She often wonders why people aren't more freaked out about plastic in the oceans. Whether in New York, the Pacific Northwest, or Glendale, California, she is grateful to call each place home. She's lucky and profoundly grateful to be a mom to a magical sprite child named Grace. To learn more about Vanessa, visit www.vanessamcgrady.com.